WITH THOSE WHO WAIT

FRANCES WILSON HUARD

WITH THOSE WHO WAIT

BY

FRANCES WILSON HUARD

AUTHOR OF "MY HOME IN THE FIELD OF HONOUR,"
"MY HOME IN THE FIELD OF MERCY," ETC.

WITH DRAWINGS BY CHARLES HUARD

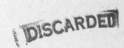

NEW YORK
GEORGE H. DORAN COMPANY

Copyright, 1918,
By George H. Doran Company

Printed in the United States of America

A MES AMIES FRANÇAISES,
HÉROINES TOUTES

ILLUSTRATIONS

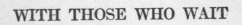

WITH THOSE WHO WAIT

WITH THOSE WHO WAIT

WITH THOSE WHO WAIT

I

ONCE upon a time there wasn't any war. In those days it was my custom to drive over to Château-Thierry every Friday afternoon. The horses, needing no guidance, would always pull up at the same spot in front of the station from which point of vantage, between a lilac bush and the switch house, I would watch for the approaching express that was to bring down our week-end guests.

A halt at the bridge head would permit our friends to obtain a bird's-eye view of the city, while I purchased a measure of fresh-caught, shiny-scaled river fish, only to be had of the old boatman after the arrival of the Paris train. Invariably there were packages to be called for at Berjot's grocery store, or Dudrumet's dry goods counter, and then H. having discovered the exact corner from which Corot painted his delightful panorama of the city, a pilgrimage to the spot almost always ensued.

A glance in passing at Jean de la Fontaine's house, a final stop at "The Elephant" on the quay to get the evening papers, and then passing through Essommes with its delightful old church, Bonneil and Romery, our joyful party would reach Villiers just in time for dinner.

A certain mystery shrouded the locality where our home was situated. Normandy, Brittany, the Châteaux of Touraine, the climate of the Riviera, have, at various seasons been more attractive, not only to foreigners, but to the Parisians themselves, so aside from the art lovers who made special trips to Rheims, there was comparatively little pleasure travelling in our immediate neighbourhood, and yet what particular portion of France is more historically renowned? Is it not on those same fertile fields so newly consecrated with our blood that every struggle for world supremacy has been fought?

It would be difficult to explain just why this neglect of the lovely East; neglect which afforded us the privilege of guiding our friends, not only along celebrated highways, but through leafy by-paths that breathed the very poetry of the XVIIth. century, and stretched, practically untrodden, through Lucy-le-Bocage, Montreuil-aux-Lions, down to the Marne and La Ferté-sous-Jouarre.

It was wonderful rolling country that rippled back from the river; abounding not only in vegetation, but in silvery green harmonies so beloved of the Barbizon master, and sympathetic even by the names of the tiny hamlets which dotted its vine-covered hills.

Our nearest dealer in agricultural machines lived in a place called Gaudelu. We called him "MacCormick" because of his absolute and loquacious partiality for those American machines, and to reach his establishment we used to pass through delightful places called le Grand Cormont, Neuilly-la-Poterie, Villers-le-Vaste.

As I write these lines (July, 1918) the station at Château-Thierry is all of that city that remains in our hands. The bridge head has become the most disputed spot on the map of Europe; "The Elephant" a heap of waste in No Man's Land, while doubtless from the very place where Corot painted his masterpiece, a

German machine gun dominating the city is belching forth its ghastly rain of steel.

That very country whose obscurity was our pride is an open book for thousands of eager allies and enemies, while on the lips of every wife and mother, from Maine to California, Belleau Woods have become words full of fearful portent. I often wonder then, if the brave Americans who are actually disputing inch by inch my home and its surroundings have ever had time to think that a little village known as "Ecoute s'il pleut," might find its English equivalent in "Hark-how-it-rains!"

Two touching accounts of the second descent upon our country have come to my hands. A little orphan peasant lad, under army age, who fled with our caravan four years since, now pointer in the French artillery—writes as follows from "Somewhere in France"—June 6, 1918:

DEAR MADAME:

Just a line to tell you I am alive and well; unfortunately I cannot say as much for my grandparents, for you doubtless know what has again befallen our country. All the inhabitants have been evacuated.

I am absolutely without news of my grand-parents. I learned to-day through a word from my brother Alfred that they had been obliged to leave home and had fled in an unknown direction. In spite of the rumour of a new invasion they did not intend to leave Villiers.

My sister left the first, with some of the young girls of the village. After twenty-four hours in Paris they were evacuated to a village in the Yonne.

My brother was obliged to go the next day, and at the present time is at Rozoy-en-Brie. I believe we made a halt there in 1914 when we fled as refugees. After three days at Rozoy, Alfred could stand it no longer, and with three companions they started home on bicycles, in order to see what had happened. They reached Villiers to find every house empty, and were almost instantly expulsed by shells. So now we are all scattered to the four winds of heaven. I am so sad when I think of my poor grand-parents, obliged to leave home and to roll along the high-roads at their age. What misery!

I am afraid our village is going to suffer much more than it did in 1914. That horde of scoundrels will spare nothing! And when will it all be over?

I hope that my letter will find you well and

happy, and I beg you to believe me gratefully and respectfully yours,

LÉON CHATELAIN
Maréchal des Logis
206ᵉ Artillerie—28ᵉ Batterie
Secteur 122.

"With the Mayor, and thanks to a neighbour's car, I was able to get away," writes Monsieur Aman Jean, the well-known painter, who had a home in Château-Thierry. "The situation was becoming unbearable and we three were the last to leave our unfortunate city. Behind us an army engineer blew up the post and telegraph office, the military buildings, the station, the store house, and finally the bridge. Our eyes were beginning to smart terribly, which announced the presence of mustard gas, and told us we had left none too soon.

"I will never forget the sight and the commotion of the road leading from Château-Thierry to Montmirail. Interminable lines of army transports on one side counterbalanced by the same number of fleeing civilians going in the opposite direction. Now and then a farm cart would pull aside to let a heavy mili-

[16]

tary truck get by, and one can hardly imagine the state of a highway that is encumbered by a double current of refugees and soldiers hastening towards the front. The painful note was made by the unfortunate civilians who had put on their Sunday clothes, the only way they had of saving them. As to the picturesque, it was added by the multitude of little donkeys trotting beneath the weight of the machine guns, and by the equipment of the Italian troops. There were bright splashes of colour here and there, together with a heroic and lamentable animation. It impressed me most violently. It was wonderfully beautiful and pathetically horrible.

"On one side old people, women and children formed a long straggling cortège; while on the other—brilliant youth constituted a homogeneous and solid mass, marching to battle with calm resolution.

"The populations of the East are astonishingly courageous and resigned. That of Château-Thierry watched the evacuation of the Government Offices, the banks, the prefecture and the post office without the slightest alarm. The retreat was well advanced ere they

dreamed of it. When finally the people realised that the enemy was at their very gates,
they moved out swiftly without any commotion."

The German onslaught at the Marne in 1914
had been terrible but brief. The life of our
entire region was practically suspended while
the Hun wreaked his vengeance, not only on
our armies, but our innocent civilians and their
possessions. Shot and shell, organised looting
and cruelty, were employed to cow the intrepid
spirit of the French, but without success.
When, finally their retreat came, hands were
quick to repair material damage, refugees
swiftly returned, and even the September rains
joined in the effort to purify the fields which
had been so ruthlessly polluted.

With the Hun on the Aisne, and a victory to
our credit, there wasn't even a pause for breath.
A new life seemed to surge forth, and all bent
their energies towards effacing every trace of
what had seemed like a hideous nightmare.
Even the Eastern Railway, which had been
closed on account of the destruction of some

[18]

seven or eight bridges over the Marne, broke all records by repairing or replacing them in eleven days' time. And while this had no direct bearing upon our situation, the moral effect of even *hearing* the train-loads of men and munitions passing through our region, was certainly surprising.

Little by little things began to assume their normal aspect. Not that they ever entirely regained it, for there was always the dull rumbling of the cannon to remind us of bygone terrors, while the establishment of several emergency hospitals in the vicinity lent an animation to the highroads, formerly dotted with private cars, but now given over entirely to ambulances and supply trucks.

As to the uniforms, they quickly became such accustomed sights that a youthful civilian would have been the novelty.

Buoyed up by the success of our armies, every one expected an early peace, and even the busiest of us began making projects for the fair future. In the odd moments of relief from my somewhat onerous hospital duties, my only pleasure and distraction was to build castles in the air, and in the eternal Winter twi-

[19]

lights I laid many a plan for a little boudoir next my bedroom, which I had long desired to see realised.

When news of H.'s safety reached me, my imagination knew no limits.

The convalescent patients from all branches of trade, who at different times had filled the rooms of the château, converted into wards, had been very deft at repairing everything in the way of furniture that the Germans had defaced or neglected to appropriate. There were many skilful carpenters and cabinet makers among them, and I saw visions of employing them at their own trade, producing both occupation, which they craved, and funds which they needed, but were too proud to accept as gifts, and what a surprise that room would be for H.!

I even pushed my collector's mania so far as to pay a visit to an old bourgeois who lived in a little city called La Ferté-Milon, quite a bit north of us. The walls of his salon were ornamented with some charming eighteenth century paper representing the ports of France, and in excellent condition. I had long coveted it for my boudoir, and in days before

[20]

the war had often dickered with him as to price. I now feared lest it should have been destroyed or disfigured, and regretted having wished to drive too keen a bargain, but on finding it intact, I am ashamed to say the collector's instinct got the better of the woman, and I used every conceivable argument to persuade him to come to my price. The old fellow was as obdurate as ever.

"But," I suggested, "don't you realise what a risk you are taking? Suppose the Germans were to get back here again before you sell it? You're much nearer the front than we! You will not only lose your money, but the world will be minus one more good thing, and we've lost too many of those already."

The withering glance with which this remark was received was as good as any discourse on patriotism.

"The Germans back here? Never! Why at the rate we're going now it will be all over before Spring and you'll see what a price my paper will fetch just as soon as peace comes!"

Peace! Peace! the word was on every lip, the thought in every heart, and yet every intelligence, every energy was bent on the prosecution of the most hateful warfare ever known. In all the universe it seemed to me that the wild animals were the only creatures really exempt from preoccupation about the fray. It might be war for man and the friends of man, but for them had come an unexpected reprieve, and even the more wary soon felt their exemption from pursuit. Man was so busy fighting his own kind that a wonderful armistice had unconsciously arisen between him and these creatures, and so birds and beasts, no longer frightened by his proximity, were indulging in a perfect revel of freedom.

During the first weeks of the conflict, the "cotton-tails," always so numerous on our estate, were simply terrified by the booming of the guns. If even the distant bombardment assumed any importance, they would disappear below ground completely, for days at a time. My old foxhound was quite disconcerted. But like all the rest of us they soon became accustomed to it, and presently displayed a self assurance and a familiarity undreamed of, save perhaps in the Garden of Eden.

It became a common sight to see a brood of partridges or pheasants strutting along the

VIEW OF CHATEAU-THIERRY

roadside like any barnyard hen and chickens, and one recalled with amazement the times when stretching themselves on their claws they would timidly and fearfully crane their necks above the grass at the sound of an approaching step.

At present they are not at all sure that man was their worst enemy. The Government having decreed that there shall be no game shooting in the army zone, weazels, pole cats and even fox have become very numerous, and covey of quail that once numbered ten and fifteen, have singularly diminished by this incursion of wild animals, not to mention the hawks, the buzzards and the squirrels.

One Autumn morning I appeared at our gateway just in time to see a neighbour's wife homeward bound, the corpses of four white hens that *Maître Renard* had borrowed from their coop, dangling from her arm. Her husband heard her coming, and on learning the motive of her wails, the imprecations brought down on the head of that fox were picturesquely profane to say the least. Presently the scene grew in violence, and then finally terminated with the assertion that the whole tragedy was the result of the Kaiser's having thrown open the German prisons and turned loose his vampires on France.

Be that as it may, there was certainly no more enchanting way of obtaining mental and physical relaxation than in wandering through those wonderful woodlands that abound in our vicinity, and which breathed so many inspirations to the Master of Fable, who at one time was their keeper. How I wish that good La Fontaine might have seen his dumb friends under present circumstances. What fantasies would he not have woven about them.

Season and the temperature were of little importance. There was never a promenade without an incident—never an incident, no matter how insignificant, that did not remind me of the peculiar phase under which every living creature was existing.

Once in the very early Spring, taking my faithful Boston bull, we stole away for a constitutional. Suddenly my little companion darted up close to the hedgerow, and on hurrying to the scene to find out the cause of this departure from her usual dignified demeanour, I found her standing face to face with a hare!

Both animals, while startled, were rooted to the spot, gazing at each other in sheer fascination of their own fearlessness. It was so amazingly odd that I laughed aloud. But even this did not break the spell. It lasted so long that presently even I became a little puzzled. Finally it was the hare who settled the question by calmly moving away, without the slightest sign of haste, leaving my bull dog in the most comical state of concern that I have ever seen.

It was about this time that *Fil-de-Fer,* our donkey, decided to abandon civilised life in favour of a more roaming career in the woods, which he doubtless felt was his only true vocation. He had fared ill at the hands of the Germans, and during the entire Winter our own boys had used him regularly to haul dead wood. This kind of *kultur* he resented distinctly, and resolved to show his disgust by becoming more independent.

First he tried it out for a day or two at a time. Then he was gone a week, and finally he disappeared altogether.

Being of sociable disposition he joined a little herd of deer which was the pride and joy of our woods, and one afternoon I came upon this motley company down by a little lick we had arranged on the brink of a tiny river that crosses our estate.

As I approached they all lifted their heads. A baby fawn, frightened, scurried into the underbrush. But the others let me come quite close, and then gently, as though to display their nimbleness and grace, bounded away mid the tender green foliage, gold splashed here and there by the fast sinking sun. *Fil-de-Fer* stood a moment undecided. Presently, lifting his hind legs high into the air he gave vent to a series of kickings and contortions which might have been taken for a comical imitation, while a second later as though realising how ridiculous he had been, he fell to braying with despair, and breaking into a gallop fled in the direction of his new found friends.

Simultaneous with *Fil-de-Fer's* disappearance came the rumour that the *Loup-garou* was abroad and was sowing panic in its wake. Just what kind of animal the *Loup-garou* might be, was somewhat difficult to ascertain. No one in our vicinity had ever seen him, and from all I could gather he seemed to be a strange sort of apocalyptic beast, gifted with horns, extraordinary force, and the especial enemy of mankind.

There was something almost uncanny in the way the peasants would look at one and lower their voices when speaking of this weird phenomenon, and presently from having suspected my innocent donkey, I began to wonder if I were not in the presence of some local popular superstition.

The rumour was still persistent, when one evening at dark there was an urgent call from Headquarters asking that we send down for four or five patients that were destined for our hospital. I do not now recall for just what reason I went alone, save for a twelve-year-old village lad, but what I do remember was the respectful moral lecture that I received from an old peasant woman who met our cart on the high-road just before we turned off into the Bois du Loup.

Night, black and starless, was upon us before we had penetrated half a mile into the woods. My youthful companion began to sing martial airs, and stimulated his courage by beating time with his feet on the bottom of the cart. A chill Autumn rain commenced to fall, tinkling against the rare leaves that now remained on the trees, blinding both horse and driver, and greatly impeding our progress. Presently I noticed that our lantern had gone out, and fearing lest we be borne down upon by some swift moving army truck, I produced a pocket lamp and descended from my seat.

A handful of damp matches, much time and good humour were consumed ere I succeeded in getting a light, and just as I swung the lantern back into place, the air was pierced by a high-pitched, blood-curdling shriek!

Le Loup . . . !

At the same moment there was a sharp crackling on the opposite side of the road, and an instant later a wild boar, followed by her young, brushed past me and darted into the obscurity.

My companion was livid. His teeth chattered audibly. He tried to pull himself together and murmured incoherent syllables. Personally, I was a bit unnerved, yet somewhat reassured. If my eyes had not deceived me, the mystery of the *Loup-garou* was now

[28]

solved. And yet I felt quite sure that wild boar were unknown in our region.

At Château-Thierry I made enquiries and from soldiers and foresters learned that heretofore inhabitants of the Ardennes forest, these animals had been driven South when man had chosen to make the firing line of their haunts; and that, prolific breeders, they were now practically a menace to the unarmed civilian. From these same lovers of nature I gathered that for the first time in their recollection sea-gulls and curlews had likewise been seen on the banks of the Marne.

While the country now abounds in newcomers, many of the old familiar birds and animals are rapidly disappearing.

Larks are rare visitors these days, and the thrush which used to hover over our vineyards in real flocks, have almost entirely vanished. The swallows, however, are our faithful friends and have never failed to return to us.

Each succeeding Spring their old haunts are in a more or less dilapidated condition according to the number of successful visits the German aviators have chosen to pay us during the Winter, and I fancy that this upsets them a trifle. For hundreds of generations they have been accustomed to nest in the pinions of certain roofs, to locate in a determined chimney, and it is a most amusing sight to see them cluster about a ruined spot and discuss the matter in strident chirpings.

Last season, after a family consultation, which lasted well nigh all the morning, and during which they made repeated visits of inspection to a certain favourite drain pipe, I suddenly saw them all lift wing and sail away towards the North. My heart sank. Something near and dear seemed to be slipping from me, and one has said *au revoir* so oft in vain. So they too were going to abandon me!

In one accustomed to daily coping with big human problems, such emotion may seem trivial, but it was perhaps this constant forced endurance that kept one up, made one almost supersensitively sentimental. Little things grew to count tremendously.

At lunch time I sauntered forth quite sad at heart, when an unexpected familiar twittering greeted my ear, and I turned northward to see my little friends circling about the stables. Life closer to the front had evidently not offered any particular advantages, and in a few days' time their constant comings and goings from certain specific points told me that they had come back to stay.

But if friend swallow may be praised for his fidelity, unfortunately not so much can be said for another familiar passerby—the wild duck. October had always seen them flocking southward, and some one of our household had invariably heard their familiar call, as at daybreak they would pass over the château on their way from the swamps of the Somme to the Marais de St. Gond. The moment was almost a solemn one. It seemed to mark an epoch in the tide of our year. Claude, Benôit, George and a decrepit gardener would abandon all work and prepare boats, guns and covers on the Marne.

Oh, the wonderful still hours just before dawn! Ah, that indescribable, intense, yet harmonious silence that preceded the arrival of our prey!

Alas, all is but memory now. Claude has fallen before Verdun, Benôit was killed on the Oise, and George has long since been reported missing.

[31]

Alone, unarmed, the old gardener and I again awaited the cry of our feathered friends, but our waiting, like that of so many others, was in vain. The wild ducks are a thing of the past. Where have they gone? No one knows, no one has ever seen them. And in the tense hush of the Autumn nights, above the distant rumble of the cannon rose only the plaintive cry of stray dogs baying at the moon.

Dogs, *mon Dieu,* I wonder how many of those poor, forgotten, abandoned creatures having strayed into our barnyard were successively washed, combed, fed, cared for and adopted.

Some of them, haunted by the spirit of unrest, remained with us but a moment; others tried us for a day, a week, and still others, appreciative of our pains, refused to leave at all.

Oh, the heart rending, lonesome, appealing look in the eyes of a poor brute that has lost home and master!

It is thus that I came into possession of an ill tempered French poodle called *Crapouillot,* which the patients in our hospital insisted on clipping like a lion with an anklet, a curl over his nose and a puff at the end of his tail.

A most detestable, unfortunate beast, always to be found where not needed, a ribbon in his hair, and despicably bad humoured.

He was succeeded by a Belgian sheep dog, baptised *Namur,* who in time gave place to one of the most hopelessly ugly mongrels I have ever seen. But the new comer was so full of life and good will, had such a comical way of smiling and showing his gleaming white teeth, that in memory of the joy caused by the Charlie Chaplin films, he was unanimously dubbed *Charlot.*

The mere sound of his name would plunge him into ecstasies of joy, accompanied by the wildest yapping and strange capers, which invariably terminated by a double somersault in the mud so anxious was he to convince us of his gratitude. Imagine then what might be obtained by a caress, or a bowl of hot soup.

Last in line, but by no means least, was a splendid English pointer, a superb, finely bred animal, who day in, day out would lie by the open fire, lost in a profound revery that terminated in a kind of sob. Poor, melancholy *Mireille,* what master was she mourning? For what home did she thus pine? How I re-

[33]

spected and appreciated her sadness. How intensely human she became.

Finally when I could resist no longer I would take her long delicate head into my hands and gently stroke it, seeking to impart my sympathy. "I know that you never can be mine," I would murmur, "that you will ever and eternally belong to him to whom you gave yourself once and entirely. But these are sad anxious days for us all; we must bear together. And so as my own dogs have often been my only consolation in like times of misery and despair, oh, how I would love to comfort you—beautiful, faithful, disconsolate Mireille!"

II

Cities, like people, seem to have souls, deep hidden and rarely ever entirely revealed. How well must one come to know them, stone by stone, highways, homes and habitants, ere they will disclose their secret. I have rejoiced too often in the splendid serenity of St. Jean des Vignes, felt too deeply the charm of those ancient streets, hoped and suffered too intensely within its confines that Soissons should not mean more to me than to the average zealous newspaper correspondent, come there but to make note of its wounds, to describe its ruins.

Fair Soissons, what is now your fate? In what state shall we find you? What ultimate destiny is reserved for your cathedral, your stately mansions, your magnificent gardens? What has become of those fifteen or sixteen hundred brave souls who loved you so well that they refused to leave you? *Qui sait?*

One arrived at Soissons in war time by long

avenues, shaded on either side by a double row
of stately elms, whose centenary branches
stretching upward formed an archway overhead. Then came the last outpost of Army
Police, a sentinel stopped you, minutely examined your passports, verified their visés, and
finally, all formalities terminated, one entered
what might have been the City of Death.

Moss and weeds had sprung up between the
cobble stone pavings; as far as eye could see
not a human soul was astir, not a familiar noise
was to be heard, not a breath of smoke stole
heavenwards from those hundreds of idle chimneys: and yet life, tenacious ardent life was
wonderfully evident here and there. A curtain
lifted as one passed, a cat on the wall, a low
distant whistle, clothes drying at a window, a
flowering plant on a balcony, sometimes a door
ajar, through which one guessed a store in
whose dimly lighted depths shadows seemed
to be moving about; all these bore witness to
an eager, undaunted existence, hidden for the
time being perhaps, but intense and victorious,
ready to spring forward and struggle anew in
admirable battles of energy and conscience.

The Hotel du Soleil d'Or offered a most

hospitable welcome. It was the only one open or rather, if one would be exact, the only one still extant. To be sure there were no panes in the windows, and ungainly holes were visible in almost all the ceilings, but the curtains were spotlessly white and the bed linen smelled sweet from having been dried in the open air.

A most appreciable surprise was the excellent *cuisine,* and as ornament to the dining-room table, between a pair of tall preserve dishes, and on either side of the central bouquet, stood an unexploded German shell. One of them had fallen on to the proprietor's bed, the second landing in the pantry, while twenty or thirty others had worked more efficiently, as could be attested by the ruins of the carriage house, stables, and what had once been a glass covered Winter garden.

On a door leading out of the office, and curiously enough left intact, one might read, *Salon de conversation.* If you were to attempt to cross the threshold, however, your eye would be instantly greeted by a most abominable heap of plaster and wreckage, and

the jovial proprietor seeing your embarrass-
ment, would explain:

"My wife and the servants are all for cleaning up, but to my mind it's better to leave
things just as they are. Besides if we put all
to rights now, when our patrons return they
will never credit half we tell them. Seeing is
believing! At any rate, it's an out of the way
place, and isn't bothering people for the time
being."

And truly enough this mania for repairing
and reconstructing, this instinct of the active
ant that immediately commences to rebuild its
hill, obliterated by some careless foot, has become as characteristic of the French.

The Sisters of St. Thomas de Villeneuve,
who were in charge of an immense hospital, had
two old masons who might be seen at all times,
trowel in hand, patching up the slightest damage to their buildings; the local manager of a
Dufayel store had become almost a fanatic on
the subject. His stock in trade consisted of
furniture, china and crockery of all kinds,
housed beneath a glass roof, which seemed to
attract the Boches' special attention, for during the four years of war just past, I believe

that scarcely a week elapsed during which he was not directly or indirectly the victim of their fire.

The effects were most disastrous, but aided by his wife and an elderly man who had remained in their employ, he would patiently recommence scrubbing, sweeping and cleaning, carefully reinstating each object or fragment thereof, in or as near as possible to its accustomed place.

It was nothing less than miraculous to survey those long lines of wardrobes that seemed to hold together by the grace of the Almighty alone; gaze upon whole rows of tables no one of which had the requisite number of legs; behold mere skeletons of chairs, whose seats or backs were missing; sofas where gaping wounds displayed the springs; huge piles of plates each one more nicked or cracked than its predecessor; series of flower pots which fell to pieces in one's hands if one were indiscreet enough to touch them.

"I don't see the point in straightening things out so often"—was my casual comment.

"Why, Madame, what on earth would we do about the inventory when peace comes, if we

were not to put a little order into our stock?"
was the immediate reply.

I was sorry I had spoken.

Among the other numerous places of interest was the store of a dealer in haberdashery
and draperies. An honest, well equipped old
fashioned French concern, whose long oak
counters were well polished from constant use.
The shelves were piled high with piece after
piece of wonderful material, but not a single
one of them had been exempt from the mur-
derous rain of steel; they were pierced, and
pierced, and pierced again.

"So pierced that there is not a length sufficient to make even a cap!" explained
Madame L., "but you just can't live in disorder all the time, and customers wouldn't like
to see an empty store. Everything we have to
sell is in the cellar!"

And true enough this subterranean existence
had long ceased to be a novelty, and had become almost a habit.

From the basement windows of every in-
habited dwelling protruded a stove pipe, and
the lower regions had gradually come to be

furnished almost as comfortably as the upper rooms in normal days. Little by little the kitchen chair and the candle had given way to a sofa and a hanging lamp; beds were set up and rugs put in convenient places.

"We live so close to the trenches that by comparison it seems like a real paradise to us," gently explained Madame Daumont, the pork butcher. Her *charcuterie* renowned far and wide for its hot meat patés, ready just at noon, had been under constant fire ever since the invasion, but had never yet failed to produce its customary ovenful at the appointed hour.

"At the time of the battle of Crouy," she confessed, "I was just on the point of shutting up shop and leaving. I'm afraid I was a bit hasty, but three shells had hit the house in less than two hours, and my old mother was getting nervous. The dough for my patés was all ready, but I hesitated. Noon came, and with it my clientèle of Officers.

" '*Eh bien, nos patés?* What does this mean!'

" 'No, gentlemen, I'm sorry, but I cannot make up my mind to bear it another day. I'm leaving in a few moments.'

" 'What? Leaving? And we who are going

out to meet death have got to face it on empty
stomachs?'

"They were right. In a second I thought
of my own husband out there in Lorraine. So
I said to them 'Come back at four o'clock and
they'll be ready.' "

And then gently, and as though to excuse
herself, she added—

"There are moments though when fear
makes you lose your head, but there doesn't
seem to be anything you can't get used to."

"You soon get used to it" was the identical
expression of a young farmer's aid who sold
fruit, vegetables and flowers beneath an archway that had once been the entrance to the
Hotel de la Clef. She had attracted my attention almost immediately, the brilliant
colours of her display, and her pink and white
complexion, standing out so fresh and clear
against the background of powder-stained
stones and chalky ruin heaps.

The next day, after an extra heavy nocturnal
bombardment, we went out in search of a
melon. A shell had shattered her impromptu
showcase, dislocated a wall on one side of the

[42]

archway, which menaced immediate collapse. In fact, the place had become untenable.

"Oh, it's such a nuisance to have to look for another sure spot," was the only lament. "Just see, there's a whole basket of artichokes gone to waste—and my roses—what a pity!"

An explosion had gutted the adjacent building leaving an immense breach opening on to the street from what had once been an office or perhaps a store-room.

"Just wait a moment," she pleaded, "until I get set up inside there. You can't half see what I've got out here."

Five minutes later I returned and explained the object of my quest.

"We've only got a very few, Madame, our garden is right in their range, and we had a whole melon patch destroyed by splinters, only day before yesterday. I had three this morning, but I sold them all to the gentleman of the artillery, and I've promised to-morrow's to the Brigade Officers. I hardly think I shall be able to dispose of any more before the end of the week. But why don't you go and see 'Père François'? He might have some."

"You mean old Père François who keeps the public gardens?"

"Yes, Madame."

"Oh, I know him very well. I've often exchanged seeds and slips with him. Does he still live where he used to?"

"I believe so."

We were not long seeking him out, and in response to our knocking his good wife opened the door.

"Oh, he's out in his garden," was her reply to our queries. "You can't keep him away from it. But he's going crazy, I think. He wants to attend to everything all by himself now. There isn't a soul left to help him, and he'll kill himself, or be killed at it as sure as I'm alive. You'll see, the shells won't miss him. He's escaped so far but he may not always be so lucky. He's already had a steel splinter in his thumb, and one of them tore a hole in his cap and in his waistcoat. That's close enough, I should think. But there's no use of my talking; he just won't listen to me. He's mad about gardening. That's what he is!"

On the old woman's assurance that we would find him by pounding hard on the gateway leading to the Avenue de la Gare, we hastened away, leaving her to babble her imprecations to a lazy tabby cat who lay sunning itself in a low window box.

The old fellow being a trifle deaf we were destined to beat a rather lengthy tattoo on the high iron gate. But our efforts were crowned with success, for presently we heard his steps approaching, his sabots crunching on the gravel path.

His face lighted up when he saw us.

"Oh, I remember you, of course I do. You're the lady who used to have the American sweet peas and the Dorothy Perkins. I know you! And the dahlias I gave you? How did they turn out?"

I grew red and sought to change the conversation. Perhaps he saw and understood.

"Come and see mine anyway!"

That sight alone would have made the trip worth while.

"I cut the grass this very morning so as they'd show off better! They're so splendid this year that I've put some in the garden at the Hotel de Ville."

Further on the *Gloire de Dijon, La France*

and *Maréchal Niels* spread forth all their magnificent odorous glory onto the balmy air of this Isle de France country, whose skies are of such exquisite delicate blue, whose very atmosphere breathes refinement.

I felt my old passion rising;—that passion which in times gone by had drawn us from our sleep at dawn, and scissors and pruning knife in hand, how many happy hours had H. and I thus spent; he at his fruit trees, I at my flower beds, cutting, trimming, scraping, clipping; inwardly conscious of other duties neglected, but held as though fascinated by the most alluring infatuation in the world—the love of nature. Here now in this delightful garden kept up by the superhuman efforts of a faithful old man, the flame kindled anew.

In an instant H. had discovered the espaliers where *Doyonné du Comice* and *Passe Cressane* were slowly but surely attaining the required degree of perfection beneath Père François' attentive care. As I stood open mouthed in wonder before the largest bush of fuchsias I had ever yet beheld, an explosion rent the air, quickly followed by a second, the latter much closer to us.

[46]

"Boche bombs! Come quick," said Père François without seeming in the least ruffled.

Led by the old man we hastened to a tiny grotto, in whose depths we could hear a fountain bubbling. Legion must have been the loving couples that have visited this spot in times gone by, for their vows of fidelity were graven in endearing terms on the stony sides of the retreat. *Léon et Marguerite pour toujours, Alice et Théodore, Georges et Germaine* were scrawled above innumerable arrow-pierced hearts.

"All things considered, I'd rather they'd send us over a shell or two than bomb us from above!" ejaculated Père François, who spoke from experience.

"It was one of those hateful things that hit my Japanese pepper tree on the main lawn, and killed our only cedar. The handsomest specimen we had here! It makes me sick every time I throw a log of it on to the fire in the Winter. I can't tell you how queer it makes me feel. Of course, it's bad enough for them to kill men who are their enemies, but think of killing trees that it takes hundreds of years to grow. What good can that do them?"

The Boche deemed at a safe distance, we visited the vegetable garden where we purchased our melon and were presented with any number of little packets containing seeds. We protested at the old man's generosity and sought to remunerate him.

"Nothing of the kind; I wouldn't think of accepting it. It's my pleasure. Why it's been ages since I had such a talk as this. I'm so glad you came. So glad for my roses too!" and he started to cut a splendid bouquet.

"I've been saying to myself every day," he continued, "Isn't it a pity that nobody should see them? But now I feel satisfied."

At the gateway we held out our hands which he took and shook most heartily, renewing his protestations of delight at our visit, and begging us to "Come again soon."

"To be happy one must cultivate his garden," murmured H., quoting Voltaire as we made off down the road. And within a day or two we again had an excellent proof of this axiom when we discovered that Abbé L. still resided in his little home whose garden extended far into the shadow of St. Jean des Vignes.

That worthy ecclesiastic gave over every moment that was not employed in the exercise of his sacred functions to the joys of archæ- ological research, and was carefully compiling a history of the churches in the arrondissement of Soissons and Château-Thierry. He had been our guest at Villiers, and I remember hav- ing made for him an imprint of two splendid low-relief tombstones which date back to the 15th century, and were the sole object and or- nament of historic interest in our little village chapel.

This history was the joy and sole distraction of his entire existence, and he never ceased collecting documents and photographs, books, plans and maps, all of which though carefully catalogued, threatened one day to take such proportions that his modest dwelling would no longer suffice to hold them.

We found him comfortably installed behind a much littered kitchen table in a room that I had heretofore known as his dining room. I was a bit struck by its disorder, and the good man was obliged to remove several piles of papers from the chairs before inviting us to be seated.

"I trust you will forgive this confusion," he begged, "but you see a shell hit my study yesterday noon, and has forced me to take refuge in this corner of the house which is certainly far safer."

"I've had an excellent occasion to work," he continued. "Our duties are very slight these days, and the extreme quiet in which we live is most propitious for pursuing the task I have undertaken."

"But, Monsieur l'Abbé," we cried. "What a paradox! And the bombardment?"

"Really, you know, I've hardly suffered from it—except when that shell struck the house the other morning. Of course, the whole edifice shook, and at one time I thought the roof was coming through upon my head. My ink bottle was upset and great streams trickled to the floor. But Divine intervention saved my precious manuscript which I was in the very act of copying, and although my notes and files were a bit disarranged, they were easily sorted and set to rights. So you see there was nothing really to deplore and God has graciously seen fit to let me continue my work. It is such a joy to be able to do so."

Strange placidity! the immediate country-side for miles around having long since been delivered up to brutal destruction, wanton waste, hideous massacre, and a goodly number of the churches of which the pious man was taking so much pains to record the history, were now but anonymous heaps of stone.

All the way home I could not refrain from philosophising on the happiness of life, perfect contentment, and the love of good. My reflections, while perhaps not particularly deep nor brilliant, were none the less imbued with a sense of gratitude to the Almighty, and filled with pity and respect for poor human nature.

It is certain that for such people, the idea of escaping the terrors, the dangers and the sight of most horrible spectacles, had not weighed an instant in the balance against the repugnance of altering life-long habits, or abandoning an assemblage of dearly beloved landscapes and faces.

Naturally enough, a certain number of commercial minded had remained behind, tempted by the possibility of abnormal gain through catering to the soldier; and to whatever had been their habitual merchandise, was soon added a stock of mandolins, accordions, cheap jewelry, kit bags, fatigue caps and calico handkerchiefs—in fact all that indispensable, gaudy trumpery that serves to attract a clientèle uniquely composed of warriors.

But, besides these merchants, there were still to be counted a certain number of well-to-do citizens, professors, government employés, priests and magistrates, all simple honest souls who had stayed because they were unable to resign themselves to an indefinite residence away from Soissons, and there was no sacrifice to which they were not resolved in advance, so long as it procured them the joy of remaining.

I accompanied the President of the local French Red Cross Chapter on a visit to a lady who was much interested in an *ouvroir,* and who lived in a splendid old mansion located near the ruins of the Palais de Justice.

The little bell tinkled several times, resounding clearly in the deathlike silence, and presently a young maid-servant made her appearance at a small door that opened in the heavy portico.

"Is Madame at home?"

"Oh, no, Madame! Why didn't Madame know that both Monsieur and Madame left for the seashore last evening? Shall I give Madame their address at Houlgate? They've been going there for the last twenty years. They will be back the first of September as usual."

"How stupid of me," exclaimed my companion. "I might have known though. We shall discover what we wish to know from Madame V."

We found the last mentioned lady and her daughter in a pretty dwelling on the boulevard Jeanne d'Arc. After presentations and greetings:

"You are not leaving town this Summer?"

"Not this season; unfortunately our country house is at present occupied by the Germans, and as the mountains are forbidden, and the sea air excites me so that I become quite ill, I fear we shall have to remain at home, for the time being at least. The garden is really delightfully cool though—we sit out there and sew all day."

I asked permission to admire the exquisite embroidered initials which both mother and daughter were working.

"I'm so glad you like them. Do you know we found that monogram on an old 18th century handkerchief? We merely enlarged it, and really feel that we have something quite unusual. But my table cloths are well worth it, they were the very last that were left at the Cour Batave. I doubt if any finer quality will ever be woven."

"Your daughter will have a wonderful trousseau."

"She will have something durable at least, Madame, a trousseau that will stand the test of time and washing," replied the good mother smiling blandly, touched by my appreciation.

"I still have sheets which came down to me from my great grand-mother, and I hope that my own great grand-sons will some day eat from this very cloth."

"But they will never guess under what strange circumstances it was hemmed and em-broidered," gently proffered the young girl

MONSIEUR S. OF SOISSONS WITH
HIS GAS MASK

raising her big blue eyes and smiling sweetly.

"Bah, what difference does that make so long as they are happy and can live in peace? That's the principal thing, the one for which we're all working, isn't it?"

Such is the spirit that pervades all France. It is simple, undemonstrative heroism, the ardent desire of a race to last in spite of all. What more imperturbable confidence in its immortality could be manifested than by this mother and daughter calmly discussing the durability of their family linen, within actual range of Teuton gunfire that might annihilate them at any moment?

As we were about to leave Monsieur S. came up the front steps. He had been out in company of a friend, making his habitual daily tour of the city. Like most middle aged, well-to-do bourgeois his attire was composed of a pair of light trousers, slightly baggy at the knee, and a bit flappy about the leg; a black cutaway jacket and a white piqué waistcoat. This classic costume usually comports a panama hat and an umbrella. Now Monsieur S. had the umbrella, but in place of the panama he had seen fit to substitute a blue steel soldier's helmet, which amazing military headgear made a strange combination with the remainder of his civilian apparel. Nevertheless he bowed to us very skilfully, and at that moment I caught sight of a leather strap, which slung over one shoulder, hung down to his waist and carried his gas mask.

For several days I laboured under the impression that this mode was quite unique, but was soon proved mistaken, for on going to the Post Office to get my mail (three carriers having been killed, there were no longer any deliveries) I discovered that it was little short of general. Several ladies had even dared risk the helmet, and the whole assembly took on a war like aspect that was quite apropos.

Thus adorned, the octogenarian Abbé de Villeneuve, his umbrella swung across his back, his cassock tucked up so as to permit him to ride a bicycle, was a sight that I shall never forget.

"Why, Monsieur le Curé, you've quite the air of a sportsman."

"My child, let me explain. You see I can no longer trust to my legs, they're too old and too rheumatic. Well then, when a bombardment sets in how on earth could I get home quickly without my bicycle?"

As visitors to the front, we were guests of the French Red Cross Society while in Soissons. The local president, whose deeds of heroism have astonished the world at large, is an old-time personal friend.

A luncheon in our honour was served on a spotless cloth, in the only room of that lady's residence which several hundred days of constant bombardment had still left intact. Yet, save for the fact that paper had replaced the window panes, nothing betrayed the proximity of the German. Through the open, vine grown casement, I could look out onto a cleanly swept little court whose centre piece of geraniums was a perfect riot of colour.

Around the congenial board were gathered our hostess, the old Curé de St. Vast, the General in command of the Brigade, his Colonel, three Aides-de-Camp, my husband and myself.

Naturally, the topic of conversation was the war, but strange as it may seem, it was we, the civilians, that were telling our friends of the different activities that were afoot and

[57]

would eventually bring the United States to the side of the Allies.

Towards the middle of the repast our enemies began sending over a few shells and presently a serious bombardment was under way. Yet no one stirred.

Dishes were passed and removed, and though oft times I personally felt that the pattering of shrapnel on the tin roof opposite was uncomfortably close, I was convinced there was no theatrical display of bravery, no cheap heroism in our companions' unconsciousness. They were interested in what was being said—*voilà tout.*

Presently, however, our hostess leaned towards me and I fancied she was about to suggest a trip cellarward, instead of which she whispered that on account of the bombardment we were likely to go without dessert since it had to come from the other side of town and had not yet arrived.

Then a shell burst quite close, and at the same time the street bell rang. The *cordon* was pulled, and through the aperture made by the backward swing of the great door, I caught sight of a ruddy cheeked, fair haired maiden

[58]

in her early teens, bearing a huge bowl of fresh cream cheese in her outstretched hands.

Steadily she crossed the court, approached the window where she halted, smiled bashfully, set down her precious burden, and timidly addressing our hostess:

"I'm sorry, Madame," said she, "so sorry if I have made you wait."

And so it goes.

I remember a druggist who on greeting me exclaimed:

"A pretty life, is it not, for a man who has liver trouble?" And yet he remained simply because it was a druggist's duty to do so when all the others are mobilised.

There was also the printer of a local daily, who continued to set up his type with one side of his shop blown out; who went right on publishing when the roof caved in, and who actually never ceased doing so until the whole structure collapsed, and a falling wall had demolished his only remaining press.

Monsieur le Préfet held counsel and deliberated in a room against whose outside wall one could hear the constant patter of machine gun bullets raining thick from the opposite bank of the river. Monsieur Muzart, the Mayor, seemed to be everywhere at once, and was always the first on the spot when anything really serious occurred.

Add to these the little dairy maids, who each morning fearlessly delivered the city's milk; or the old fellow on whom had devolved the entire responsibility of the street-cleaning department and who went about, helmet clad, attending to his chores, now and then shouting a hearty *"Whoa Bijou,"* to a faithful quadruped who patiently dragged his dump cart, and over whose left ear during the entire Summer, was tied a bunch of tri-colour field flowers.

I had almost forgotten to mention two extraordinary old women, whom I came upon seated out in a deserted street, making over a mattress, while gently discussing their private affairs. It was the end of a warm July afternoon. A refreshing coolness had begun to rise from the adjacent river, and in the declining sunlight I could see great swarms of honey bees hovering about a climbing rose bush whose fragrant blossoms hung in huge clusters over the top of a convent wall near by. I could not resist the temptation. Pressed by the desire to possess I stepped forward and was about to reach upward when a masculine voice, whose owner was hidden somewhere near my elbow called forth:

"Back, I say! Back! you're in sight!"

I quickly dived into the shadow for cover just in time to hear the bullets from a German machine gun whizz past my ear!

"You can trust them to see everything," murmured one of the old women, not otherwise disturbed. "But if you really want some roses just go around the block and in by the back gate, Madame."

How in the presence of such calm can we believe in war?

Ah, France! elsewhere perhaps there may be just as brave—but surely none more sweetly!

III

THE little village was just behind the lines. The long stretch of roadway, that following the Aisne finally passed through its main street, had been so thoroughly swept by German fire that it was as though pockmarked by ruts and shell holes, always half full of muddy water.

A sign to the left said—

Chemin défilé de V.—

There could be no choice; there was but to follow the direction indicated, branch out onto a new highway which, over a distance of two or three miles, wound in and out with many strategic contortions; a truly military route whose topography was the most curious thing imaginable. If by accident there happened to be a house in its way it didn't take the trouble to go *around,* but *through* the edifice.

One arrived thus in the very midst of the village, having involuntarily traversed not only the notary's flower garden, but also his drawing-room, if one were to judge by the quality of the now much faded wall paper, and the empty spots where portraits used to hang.

The township had served as target to the German guns for many a long month, and was seriously *amoché*, as the saying goes. "Coal scuttles" by the hundred had ripped the tiles from almost every roof. Huge breaches gaped in other buildings, while some of them were completely levelled to the ground. Yet, in spite of all, moss, weeds and vines had sprung up mid the ruins, adding, if possible, the picturesque to this scene of desolation. One robust morning glory I noted had climbed along a wall right into the soot of a tumble-down chimney, and its fairylike blossoms lovingly entwined the iron bars whereon had hung and been smoked many a succulent ham.

The territorials (men belonging to the older army classes), had installed their mess kitchens in every convenient corner: some in the open court-yards and others beneath rickety stables and sheds, where the sunlight piercing the gloom caught the dust in its rays and made it seem like streams of golden powder, whose brightness enveloped even the most sordid nooks and spread cheer throughout the dingy atmosphere.

Fatigue squads moved up and down the road, seeking or returning with supplies, while those who were on duty, pick and shovel in hand, moved off to their work in a casual, leisurely manner one would hardly term military.

Of civilians there remained but few. Yet civilians there were, and of the most determined nature: "hangers-on" who when met in this vicinity seemed almost like last specimens of an extinct race, sole survivors of the world shipwreck.

At the moment of our arrival an old peasant woman was in the very act of scolding the soldiers, who to the number of two hundred and fifty (a whole company) filled to overflowing her modest lodgings, where it seemed to me half as many would have been a tight squeeze. It was naturally impossible for her to have an eye on all of them. In her distress she took me as witness to her trials.

"Just see," she vociferated, "they trot through my house with their muddy boots, they burn my wood, they're drying up my well, and on top of it all they persist in smoking in my hay-loft, and the hay for next Winter is in! Shouldn't you think their Officers would look after them? Why, I have to be a regular watch-dog, I do!"

"That's all very well, mother," volunteered a little dried up Corporal. "But how about *their* incendiary shells? You'll get one of them sooner or later. See if you don't!"

"If it comes, we'll take it; we've seen lots worse than that! Humph! That's no reason why you should mess up a house that belongs to your own people, is it? I'd like to know what your wife would say if she caught you smoking a pipe in her hay loft?"

Shouts of laughter from the culprits. Then a tall, lean fellow, taking her side, called out:

"She's right, boys, she had a hard enough job getting the hay in all by herself. Put out your pipes since that seems to get on her nerves. Now then, mother, there's always a way of settling a question between honest people. We won't smoke in your hay any more; that is, provided you'll sell us fresh vegetables for our mess."

The old woman was trapped and had to surrender, which she did, but most ungraciously, all the while moaning that she would more than likely die of starvation the following Winter. So a moment later the group dispersed on hearing the news that the "Auto-bazaar" had arrived.

This auto-bazaar certainly contained more treasures than were ever dreamed of in ancient Golconda. There was everything the soldier's heart might desire, from gun grease and cigarette paper down to wine and provisions; the whole stored away in a literal honey-comb of shelves and drawers with which the sides were lined.

The men all hurried forward. Loaded with water bottles, their hands full of coppers, they clustered about it.

From his dominating position at the rear end of the truck, the store-keeper announced:

"No more pork pie left!"

This statement brought forth several indignant oaths from the disappointed.

"It's always that way, they're probably paid to play that joke on us. It was the same story last time! We'll send in a complaint. See if we don't."

But these grumblings were soon outvoiced by the announcement—

"Plenty of head-cheese and camembert. Now then, boys, who's ready?"

The effect was instantaneous.

Smiles broke out on every countenance. The good news was quickly spread abroad, and presently the sound of plates and dishes, clinking cups, and joyful laughter recalled a picnic which we had organised in the vicinity, one warm July afternoon some four years ago.

A military band rehearsing a march in an open field just behind us added life and gaiety to the scene, and reminded me of the "Merry-go-round," the chief attraction of that defunct country fair, and upon which even the most dignified of our friends had insisted riding.

After all, could it be possible that this was the very midst of war? Was it such a terrible thing, since the air fairly rung with merriment?

"Make room there," called a gruff voice, not far distant.

"Stand aside! Quick now!"

The crowd parted, and a couple of stretcher bearers with their sad human burden put an end to my soliloquy. My afternoon was stained with blood. On their litter they bore a lad whose bloodless lips, fluttering eyelids, and heaving breast, bespoke unutterable suffering.

One must have actually witnessed such sights to realise the enormity of human agony, grasp the torment that a stupid bit of flying steel can inflict upon a splendid human frame—so well, so happy, so full of hope but a second since. Oh, the pity of it all!

"Who is it?" the men whisper.

"Belongs to the 170th. They replaced us. He was caught in the *Boyau des Anglais*."

"That's a wicked spot, that is!"

"Is he one of ours?" questioned a man from an upper window, stopping an instant in the act of polishing his gun.

"No," answers some one.

The enquirer recommenced his work, and with it the refrain of his song, just where he had left off.

"*Sur les bords de la Riviera*," sang he blithely.

Little groups formed along the wayside. Seated on the straw they finished their afternoon meal, touching mugs, and joking together. Near them the artillerymen greased and verified their axles; others brushed and curried the horses. In one spot a hair dresser had set up his tonsorial parlor in the open, and his customers formed in line awaiting their turns.

Further on the *permissionaires* blacked their boots and furbished their raiment, making ready to leave for home. Swarms of humming birds and bees clustered about a honey-suckle vine which clung to the fragments of a fence near by, and whose fragrance saturated the air.

The friend, whose regiment number we had recognised, and stopped to see, came up from behind and touched me on the shoulder.

"Well, of all things! What on earth are you doing here?"

We explained our mission, and then inquired about mutual acquaintances.

"Pistre? Why he's with the munitions in the 12xth. We'll go over and see him. It's not far. But hold on a minute, isn't Lorrain a friend of yours?"

We acquiesced.

[69]

"Well, his son's my lieutenant. I'll go and get him. He'd be too sorry to miss you."

He disappeared and a few moments later returned followed by his superior, a handsome little nineteen year old officer, who came running up, his pipe in his mouth, his drinking cup still in his hand. The lad blushed scarlet on seeing us, for he doubtless recalled, as did I, the times not long gone by, when I used to meet him at a music teacher's, his long curls hanging over his wide sailor collar.

The idea that this mere infant should have command over such a man as our friend Nourrigat, double his age, and whose life of work and struggle had been a marvel to us all, somewhat shocked me.

I think the little chap felt it, for he soon left us, pleading that he must be present at a conference of officers.

"A brave fellow and a real man," commented Nourrigat, as the boy moved away. "His whole company has absolute confidence in him. You can't imagine the calm and prestige that kid possesses in the face of danger. He's the real type of leader, he is! And let me tell you, he's pretty hard put sometimes."

And then in a burst of genuine enthusiasm, he continued:

"It's wonderful to be under twenty, with a smart little figure, a winsome smile, and a gold stripe on your sleeve. The women willingly compare you to the Queen's pages, or Napoleon's handsome hussars. That may be all very well in a salon, or in the drawings you see in 'La Vie Parisienne,' but it takes something more than that to be a true officer. He's got to know the ropes at playing miner, bombarder, artilleryman, engineer, optician, accountant, caterer, undertaker, hygienist, carpenter, mason—I can't tell you what all. And in each particular job he's got to bear the terrible responsibility of human lives; maintain the discipline and the moral standard, assure the cohesion of his section. Moreover, he's called upon to receive orders with calm and reserve under the most difficult and trying circumstances, must grasp them with lightning speed and execute them according to rules and tactics. A moment of hesitancy or forgetfulness, and he is lost. The men will no longer follow him. I tell you it isn't everybody that's born to be a leader!"

[71]

"But, was he educated for the career?" we questioned.

"I don't think so. I imagine he's just waiting for the end of the war to continue his musical studies—that is if he comes out alive."

"And you?"

"I? Why I've no particular ambition. I suppose I could have gone into the Camouflage Corps if I'd taken the trouble to ask. But what's the use of trying to shape your own destiny?"

"You've gotten used to this life?"

"Not in the least. I abominate and adore it all in the same breath. Or, to be more explicit, I admire the men and abhor the military pictures, the thrilling and sentimental ideas of the warrior with which the civilian head is so generously crammed. I love military servitude, and the humble life of the men in the ranks, but I have a genuine horror of heroes and their sublimity.

"Just look over there," he went on, waving his hand towards a long line of seated *poilus* who were peacefully enjoying their pipes, while wistfully watching the smoke curl upward. "Just look at them, aren't they

[72]

splendid? Why they've got faces like the 'Drinkers' in the Velasquez picture. See that little fellow rolling his cigarette? Isn't he the image of the Bacchus who forms the centre of the painting? That's Brunot, and he's thinking about all the god-mothers whose letters swell out his pockets. He can't make up his mind whether he prefers the one who lives in Marseilles and who sent him candied cherries and her photograph; or the one from Laval who keeps him well supplied with devilled ham which he so relishes. The two men beside him are Lemire and Lechaptois—both peasants. When they think, it's only of their farms and their wives. That other little thin chap is a Parisian bookkeeper. I'd like to bet that he's thinking of his wife, and only of her. He's wondering if she's faithful to him. It's almost become an obsession. I've never known such jealousy, it's fairly killing him.

"That man Ballot, just beyond"—and our friend motioned up the line—"that man Ballot would give anything to be home behind his watch-maker's stand. In a moment or so he'll lean over and begin a conversation with his neighbour Thevenet. They've only one topic, and it's been the same for two years. It's angling. They haven't yet exhausted it.

"All of them at bottom are heartily wishing it were over; they've had enough of it. But they're good soldiers, just as before the war they were good artisans. The *métier* is sacred—as are the Family and Duty. 'The Nation, Country, Honour' are big words for which they have a certain repugnance.

" 'That's all rigmarole that somebody hands you when you've won the Wooden Cross and a little garden growing over your tummy,' is the way they put it in their argot. 'The Marseillaise, the Chant du Depart are all right for the youngsters, and the reviews—and let me tell you, the reviews take a lot of furbishing and make a lot of dust. That's all they really amount to.'

"When they sing, it's eternally 'The Mountaineers' who, as you know, are always 'there,' 'Sous les Ponts de Paris,' 'Madelon' and other sentimental compositions, and if by accident, in your desire to please, you were prone to compare them to the heroes of Homer, it's more than likely your pains would be rewarded by the first missile on which they could lay their

[74]

hands and launch in your direction. They will not tolerate mockery.

"No," he went on, filling his pipe, and enunciating between each puff. "No, they are neither supermen nor heroes; no more than they are drunkards or foul mouthed blackguards. No, they are better than all that—they are men, real men, who do everything they do well; be it repairing a watch, cabinet-making, adding up long columns of figures or peeling potatoes, mounting guard, or going over the top! They do the big things as though they were small, the small things as though they were big!

"Two days ago the captain sent for two men who had been on patrol duty together. He had but one decoration to bestow and both chaps were in hot discussion as to who should *not* be cited for bravery.

" 'Now, boys, enough of this,' said the captain. 'Who was leading, and who first cut the German barbed wire?'

" 'Dubois.'

" 'Well then, Dubois, what's all this nonsense? The cross is yours.'

" 'No, sir, if you please, that would be idiotic!

[75]

I'm a foundling, haven't any family. What's a war cross more or less to me? Now Paul here keeps a café; just think of the pleasure it will give his clientèle to see him come back decorated.'

"The captain who knows his men, understood Dubois' sincerity, and so Paul got the medal.

"I believe it was Péguy who said that 'Joan of Arc has the same superiority over other saints, as the man who does his military service has over those who are exempt.' But 'it's only the soldiers who really understand that, and when they say *On les aura,* it means something more from their lips, 'than when uttered by a lady over her tea-cups, or a reporter in his newspaper."

During this involuntary monologue we had strolled along the road which Nourrigat had originally indicated as the direction of our friend Pistre. Presently he led us into the church, a humble little village sanctuary. A shell had carried away half the apse, and sadly damaged the altar. The belfry had been demolished and the old bronze bell split into four pieces had been carefully fitted together by

A VILLAGE ON THE FRONT

some loving hand, and stood just inside the doorway.

St. Anthony of Padua had been beheaded, and of St. Roch there remained but one foot and half his dog. Yet, a delightful sensation of peace and piety reigned everywhere. From the confessional rose the murmur of voices, and the improvised altar was literally buried beneath garlands of roses.

In what had once been a chapel, a soldier now sat writing. His note books were spread before him on a table, a telephone was at his elbow.

Chalk letters on a piece of broken slate indicate that this is the *"Bureau de la 22ᵉ."*

An old bent and withered woman, leaning on a cane, issued from this office-chapel as we approached.

"Why that's mother Tesson," exclaimed Nourrigat. "Good evening, mother; how's your man to-day?"

"Better, sir. Much better, thank you. They've taken very good care of him at your hospital."

The old couple had absolutely refused to evacuate their house. The Sous-Prefet, the

[77]

Prefet, all the authorities had come and insisted, but to no avail.

"We've lost everything," she would explain. "Our three cows, our chickens, our pigs. Kill us if you like, but don't force us to leave home. We worked too hard to earn it!"

And so they had hung on as an oyster clings to its rock. One shell had split their house in twain, another had flattened out the hayloft. The old woman lay on her bed crippled with rheumatism, her husband a victim of gall stones. Their situation was truly most distressing.

But there were the soldiers. Not any special company or individual—but the soldiers, the big anonymous mass—who took them in charge and passed them on from one to another.

"We leave father and mother Tesson to your care," was all they said to the new comers as they departed. But that was sufficient, and so the old couple were nursed, clothed and fed by those whom one would suppose had other occupations than looking after the destitute.

Three times the house was brought to earth. Three times they rebuilt it. The last time they even put in a stove so that the old

woman would not have to bend over to reach
her hearth. New beds were made and installed,
the garden dug and planted. The old man was
operated upon at the Division Hospital, and
when he became convalescent they shared the
contents of their home packages with him.

Who were they? This one or that one?
Mother Tesson would most surely have been at
a loss to name the lad who returned from his
furlough bringing two hens and a rooster to
start her barnyard. She vaguely remembered
that he was from the south, on account of his
accent, and that he must have travelled across
all France with his cage of chickens in his
hand.

They entered her home, smoked a pipe by
her fireside, helped her to wash the dishes or
shell peas; talked a moment with her old man
and left, saying *au revoir.*

Another would come back greeting her
with a cordial *"Bonjour, mère Tesson."*

"Good day, my son," she would reply.

And it was this constantly changing new
found son who would chop wood, draw water
from the well, write a letter that would exempt

[79]

them from taxes, or make a demand for help from the American Committees.

Thus the aged pair had lived happily, loved and respected, absolutely without want, and shielded from all material worry. And when some poor devil who has spent four sleepless nights in the trenches, on his return steals an hour or two from his well earned, much craved sleep, in order to hoe their potato patch, one would doubtless be astonished to hear such a man exclaim by way of excuse for his conduct—

"Oh, the poor old souls! Just think of it! At their age. What a pity."

We found Pistre making a careful toilet with the aid of a tin pail full of water.

"This is a surprise, on my soul!"

We hastened to give him news of his family and friends.

Presently he turned towards Nourrigat.

"How about your regiment? Stationary?"

"I fancy so. We were pretty well thinned out. We're waiting for reinforcements."

"What's become of Chenu, and Morlet and Panard?"

"Gone! all of them."

"Too bad! They were such good fellows!"

And our friends smiled, occupied but with the thought of the living present. Paris, their friends, their families, their professions, all seemed to be forgotten, or completely over-shadowed by the habitual daily routine of marches and halts, duties and drudgery. They were no longer a great painter and a brilliant barrister. They were two soldiers; two atoms of that formidable machine which shall conquer the German; they were as two monks in a monastery—absolutely oblivious to every worldly occupation.

We understand, we feel quite certain that they will be ours again—but later—when this shall all be over—if God spares them to return.

At that same instant two boys appeared at the entrance to the courtyard. They may have been respectively ten and twelve years of age. The perspiration trickled from their faces, and they were bending beneath the weight of a huge bundle each carried on his back.

"Hello, there, fellows," called one of them.

A soldier appeared on the threshold.

"Here Lefranc—here are your two boxes of sardines, and your snuff. There isn't any more plum jam to be had. Oh, yes, and here's your writing paper."

The child scribbled something in an old account book.

"That makes fifty-three sous," he finally announced.

Other soldiers now came up.

The boys were soon surrounded by a group of eager gesticulating *poilus*.

"Oh, shut up, can't you? How can a fellow think if you all scream at once? Here—Mimile"—and he turned to his aid. "Don't you give 'em a thing."

Then the tumult having subsided, he continued—

"Now then, your names, one at a time—and don't muddle me when I'm trying to count!"

Pistre quickly explained that this phenomenon was Popaul called "Business"—and Mimile, his clerk, both sons of a poor widow who washed for the soldiers. In spite of his tender years "Business" had developed a tendency for finance that bespoke a true captain of industry. He had commenced by selling the men newspapers, and then having saved enough to buy first one and then a second bicycle, the brothers went twice a day to Villers Cotterets, some fifteen miles distant, in quest of the orders given them by the soldiers. At first the dealers tried to have this commerce prohibited, but as the lads were scrupulously honest, and their percentage very modest, the Commandant not only tolerated, but protected them.

Mimile was something of a Jonah, having twice been caught by bits of shrapnel, which necessitated his being cared for at the dressing station.

"All his own fault too," exclaimed Business, shrugging his shoulders. "He's no good at diving. Doesn't flatten out quick enough. Why I used to come right over the road last Winter when the bombardment was on full tilt. I was then working for the Legion and the Chasseurs. No cinch let me tell you! It used to be—'Popaul here—Popaul there— where's my tobacco? How about my eau-de-Cologne?' There wasn't any choice with those fellows. It was furnish the goods or bust—and

I never lost them a sou's worth of merchandise either!"

Business knew everything and everybody; all the tricks of the trade, all the tricks of the soldiers. He had seen all the Generals, and all the Armies from the British to the Portuguese.

He had an intimate acquaintance with all the different branches of warfare, as well as a keen memory for slang and patois. He nourished but one fond hope in his bosom—a hope which in moments of expansion he imparts, if he considers you worthy of his confidence.

"In four years I'll volunteer for the aviation corps."

"In four years? That's a long way off, my lad. That's going some, I should say," called a *poilu* who had overheard the confession.

"Look here, Business, did I hear you say it won't be over in four years?" asked another.

"Over? Why, it'll have only just begun. It was the Americans on the motor trucks who told me so, and I guess they ought to know!"

We watched him distribute his packages, make change and take down his next day's orders, in a much soiled note-book, and with the aid of a stubby pencil which he was obliged to

[84]

wet every other letter. When he had finished
a soldier slipped over towards him.

"I say, Paul," he called out to him, "would
you do us the honour of dining with us? We've
got a package from home. Bring your brother
with you."

Business was touched to the quick.

"I'm your man," he answered. "And with
pleasure. But you must let me furnish the
aperatif."

"Just as you say, old man."

Brusquely turning about, the future trades-
man sought for his clerk who had disappeared.

"Mimile," he shouted, "Mimile, I say, run
and tell mamma to iron our shirts and put some
polish on our shoes. I'll finish to-day's job by
myself."

IV

NOT satisfied with the havoc wrought in Soissons and other cities of the front, the Boche is now trying to encircle the head of Paris with the martyr's crown. The capital, lately comprised in the army zone, has been called upon to pay its blood tax, and like all the other heroic maimed and wounded, has none the less retained its good humour, its confidence and its serenity.

"It will take more than that to prevent us from going to the cafés," smiled an old Parisian, shrugging his shoulders.

And this sentiment was certainly general if one were to judge by the crowd who literally invaded the *terrasses* between five and seven, and none of whom seemed in the least preoccupied or anxious.

Aperatifs have long since ceased to be anything save pleasant remembrances—yet the custom itself has remained strong as a tradition. Absinthes, bitters and their like have not only been abolished, but replaced—and by what? Mineral waters, fruit syrups and tea! The waiters have been metamorphosed into herbalists. Besides, what am I saying, there are really no more waiters, save perhaps a few decrepit specimens whom flatfoot has relegated beyond the name, their waddling so strangely resembles that of ducks. All the others are serving—at the front.

From my seat I could see two ferocious looking, medal bespangled warriors ordering, the one a linden flower and verbena, the other camomile with mint leaf. And along with the cups, saucers and tea-pots, the waiter brought a miniature caraffe, which in times gone by contained the brandy that always accompanied an order of coffee. At present its contents was extract of orange flower!

There may be certain smart youth who brag about having obtained kirsch for their *tilleul,* or rum in their tea, but such myths are scarcely credited.

Naturally there is the grumbling element who claim that absinthe never hurt any one, and cite as example the painter Harpignies, who lived to be almost a hundred, having ab-

[87]

sorbed on the average of two a day until the very last.

But all have become so accustomed to making sacrifices that even this one is passed off with a smile. What can one more or less mean now? Besides, the women gave up pastry, didn't they?

One joked the first time one ordered an infusion or a lemon vichy, one was even a bit disgusted at the taste. And then one got used to it, the same as one is ready to become accustomed to anything; to trotting about the darkened streets, to going to bed early, to getting along without sugar, and even to being bombed.

There is a drawing by Forain which instantly obtained celebrity, and which represents two French soldiers talking together in the trenches.

"If only they're able to stick it out!"

"Who?"

"The civilians!"

And now at the end of four long years it may be truly said of the civilian that he has "seen it through." Not so gloriously, perhaps, but surely quite as magnificently as his brothers at the front.

In a country like France, where all men must join the army, the left-behind is not an indifferent being; he is a father, a brother, a son, or a friend; he is that feverish creature who impatiently waits the coming of the postman, who lives in a perpetual state of agony, trembles for his dear ones, and at the same time continues his business, often doubling, even trebling his efforts so as to replace the absent, and still has sufficient sense of humour to remark:

"In these days when every one is a soldier, it's a hard job to play the civilian."

Last summer an American friend said to me:

"Of course, there are some changes, but as I go about the streets day in and day out, it hardly seems as though Paris were conscious of the war. It is quite unbelievable."

But that very same evening when slightly after eleven, Elizabeth and I sauntered up the darkened, deserted Faubourg St. Honoré—

"Think," she said, catching my arm, "just think that behind each and every one of those

[89]

façades there is some one suffering, hoping, weeping, perhaps in secret! Think of the awful moment when all the bells shall solemnly toll midnight, every stroke resounding like a dirge in the souls of those who are torn with anxiety, who crave relief, and patiently implore a sleep that refuses to come."

The soldiers know it, know but too well the worth of all the energies expended without thought of glory; appreciate the value of that stoicism which consists in putting on a bold front and continuing the every-day life, without betraying a trace of sorrow or emotion.

Many a husband is proud of his wife, many a brother of his sister, and many a son of his father and his mother.

Even those, who all things considered would seem the farthest from the war, suffer untold tortures. How often last autumn did H. and I pay visits to old artist friends, men well into the sixties with no material worries, and no one at the front; only to find them alone in one corner of their huge studios, plunged in profound reveries, and utterly unconscious of the oncoming night, or the rain that beat against the skylights.

[90]

"I know, I know, it's all very well to shake yourself and say you must work. It's easy enough to recall that in 1870 Fantin Latour shut himself up and painted fruit and flowers, and by emulation, buoyed up perhaps by this precedent, you sit down and sketch a still life. What greater joy than to seek out a harmony, find the delicate suave tones, and paint it in an unctuous medium. Yes, it's a joy, but only when head and heart are both in it! The museums too, used to be a source of untold pleasure, but even if they were open you wouldn't go, because the head and the heart are 'Out there' where that wondrous youth is being mowed down—'Out there' where lies our every hope, 'Out there' where we would like to be, all of us! 'Tis hardly the moment to paint ripe grapes and ruddy apples, and to feel that you're only good for that! It's stupid to be old!"

And many, many a dear old man has passed away, unnoticed. When one asks the cause of a death friends shrug their shoulders,

"We scarcely know, some say one thing, some another—perhaps the war!"

"In proportion you'll find that there are as

many deaths on the Boulevard as in the trenches," said our friend, Pierre Stevens, on returning from Degas' funeral.

I would you might go with me, all you who love France, into one of those Parisian houses, where after dinner when the cloth has been removed, the huge road maps are spread out on the dining-room table, and every one eagerly bends over them with bated breath, while the latest *communiqué* is read. Fathers, mothers, grandmothers, and little children, friends and relatives, solemnly, anxiously await the name of *their secteurs*—the *secteurs* where *their* loved ones are engaged. How all the letters are read, re-read and handed about, each one seeking a hidden sense, the meaning of an allusion; how dark grows every brow when the news is not so good—what radiant expanse at the word victory.

And through fourteen hundred long days this same scene has been repeated, and no one has ever quailed.

The theatres have cellars prepared to receive their audiences in case of bombardment, and one of our neighbours, Monsieur Walter, has just written asking permission in my absence to build an armoured dug-out in the hallway of my home.

"It is precisely the organisation of this dug-out that prompts my writing to you, *chère Madame.*

"So much bronchitis and so many other ills have been contracted in cellars, that I hesitate to take my children down there; but on the other hand, I dare not leave them upstairs, where they would be altogether too exposed. It is thus that I conceived the idea of asking your permission to transform into a sort of 'Dug-out dormitory'—(if I may be permitted the expression) the little passage way, which in your house separates the dining-room from the green room. To have something absolutely safe, it would be necessary to give the ceiling extra support, then set steel plates in the floor of the little linen room just above and sandbag all the windows.

"Naturally, I have done nothing pending your consent. Useless to say, we will put everything in good order if you return, unless you should care to use the dug-out yourself. My wife and I shall anxiously await your reply."

And this in Paris, June 28th, 1918!

I do not know what particular epoch in world war events served as inspiration to the author of a certain ditty, now particularly popular among the military. But decidedly his injunction to

"Pack all your troubles in an old kit bag,
And smile, smile, smile,"

has been followed out to the letter, in the case of the Parisian, who has also added that other virtue "Patience" to his already long list of qualities.

With the almost total lack of means of communication, a dinner downtown becomes an expedition, and a theatre party a dream of the future.

During the Autumn twilights, on the long avenues swept by the rain, or at street corners where the wind seizes it and turns it into miniature water spouts, one can catch glimpses of the weary, bedraggled Parisian, struggling beneath a rebellious umbrella, patiently waiting for a cab. He has made up his mind to take the first that goes by. There can be no question of discrimination. Anything will be welcome. Yes, anything, even one of those evil-smelling antiquated hackneys drawn by a decrepit brute who will doubtless stumble and fall before having dragged you the first five hundred yards, thereby bringing down the pitiless wrath of his aged driver, not only on his own, but your head.

Taxis whizz by at a rate which leads one to suppose that they had a rendezvous with dame Fortune. Their occupants are at the same time objects of envy and admiration, and one calls every latent cerebral resource to his aid, in order to guess where on earth they were to be found empty. And how consoling is the disdainful glance of the chauffeur who, having a fare, is hailed by the unfortunate, desperate pedestrian that has a pressing engagement at the other end of town.

If one of them ever shows signs of slowing up, it is immediately pounced upon and surrounded by ten or a dozen damp human beings.

Triumphantly the driver takes in their humble, supplicating glances (glances which have never been reproduced save in pictures of the Martyrs), and then clearing his throat he questions:

"First of all I've got to know where you want to go. I'm bound for Grenelle."

Nobody ever wants to go to Grenelle.

If some one tactfully suggests the Avenue de Messine, he is instantly rebuffed by a steady stare that sends him back, withered, into the second row of the group. A shivering woman, taking all her courage into her hands, suggests the Palais d'Orsay, but is ignored while a man from behind calls forth "Five francs if you'll take me to the Avenue du Bois."

The chauffeur's glance wavers, it seems possible that he might entertain the proposal. The gentleman steps forward, already has his hand on the door handle, when from somewhere in the darkness, helmet clad, stick in his hand, kit bag over one shoulder, a *poilu permission-aire* elbows his way through the crowd. There is no argument, he merely says,

"Look here, old man, I've got to make the 6.01 at the Gare du Nord; drive like hell!"

"You should worry. We'll get there."

Now, the Gare du Nord is certainly not in the direction of Grenelle. On the contrary

[96]

it is diametrically opposite, geographically speaking. But nobody seems to mind. The chauffeur is even lauded for his patriotic sentiments, and one good-hearted, bedraggled creature actually murmurs:

"I only hope the dear fellow does make it!"

"What does it matter if we do have to wait a bit—that's all we've really got to do, after all," answers an elderly man moving away.

"It would be worse than this if we were in the trenches," chimes in some one else.

"My son is in water up to his waist out there in Argonne," echoes a third, as the group disbands.

And yet people do go to the theatre.

Gémier has made triumphant productions, with the translations of the Shakesperean Society, and true artist that he is, has created sensational innovations by way of *mise-en-scène* in the "Merchant of Venice" and "Anthony and Cleopatra."

It's a far cry now to the once all too popular staging à la Munich.

Lamy and Le Gallo were excruciatingly funny in a farce called "My God-son," but the real type of theatrical performance which is

[97]

unanimously popular, which will hold its own to the very end, is the Review.

How on earth the authors manage to scrape up enough comic subjects, when sadness is so generally prevalent, and how they succeed in making their public laugh spontaneously and heartily, without the slightest remorse or *arrière pensée,* has been a very interesting question to me.

Naturally, their field is limited, and there are certain subjects which are tabooed completely; so the trifling event, the ridiculous side of Parisian life, have come to the fore. Two special types, the slacker and the profiteer, or *nouveau riche,* are very generally and very thoroughly maltreated. If I am any judge, it is the *embusqué,* who is the special pet, and after him come the high cost of living, the lack of fuel, the obscurity of the streets, the length of women's skirts, etc.—all pretexts for more or less amusing topical songs.

As to the war itself, they have made something very special of it. Thanks to them the trenches become a very delightful spot populated by a squadron of nimble footed misses,

who, booted, spurred, helmet-crowned and costumed in horizon blue, sing of the heroism and
the splendid good humour of the *poilu* while
keeping time to a martial rhythm.

There is invariably a heavy comedian who
impersonates the jovial *chef*—preparing a
famous sauce in which to dish up "Willy" the
day he shall be captured; the soldier on furlough who is homesick for the front; the
wounded man who stops a moment to sing
(with many frills and flourishes) the joys of
shedding one's blood for his country.

Attacks are made to well known accom-
paniments—Bombardments perpetrated in
the wings by the big bass drum, and both
though symbolic, are about as unreal as possible.

Nobody is illusioned, no one complains. On
the contrary, they seem delighted with the
show they have paid to see. Furthermore,
the better part of the audience is composed of
soldiers, wounded men, convalescents, and *permissionaires,* and they all know what to expect.

Near me sat two of the latter—healthy looking lads, wind burned and tanned, their uniforms sadly faded and stained, their helmets

scarred and indented. Both wore the *Croix de Guerre,* and the *Fourragère* or shoulder strap, showing the colours of the military medal, which at that time being quite a novelty, caught and held the eyes of all who surrounded them.

From scraps of their conversation I learned that they had left the battle front of the Somme that very morning, were merely crossing Paris, taking a midnight train which would land them home some time the following day.

I even managed to gather that their papers had reached them at the very moment when they came out of the trenches, that they had not even had time to brush up, so great was their fear of missing the last train.

Less than twenty-four hours ago, then, they had really been in it—standing out there in the mud, surrounded by rats and the putrid odour of dead bodies, the prey not only of the elements, but of enemy bombs and shells, expecting the end at any instant; or curled up, half frozen in a humid, slimy dug-out, not long enough to permit stretching out—scarcely deep enough to be called a shelter.

Would they not be disgusted? Ready to

protest against this disfigured travesty of *their* war?

I feel quite certain they never gave it a thought. Blissfully installed in their comfortable orchestra seats they didn't intend to miss a word of the entire performance. And when finally in an endless chain of verses, a comedian, mimicking a *poilu* with his kit on his back, recited his vicissitudes with the army police, and got mixed up in his interpretation of R.A.T., G.Q.G.—etc., they burst into round after round of applause, calling and recalling their favourite, while their sides shook with laughter, and the tears rolled down their cheeks.

These same faces took on a nobly serious aspect, while a tall, pale, painted damsel draped in a peplum, evoked in ringing tones the glorious history of the tri-colour. I looked about me—many a manly countenance was wrinkled with emotion, and women on all sides sniffed audibly. It was then that I understood, as never before, what a philosopher friend calls "the force of symbols."

An exact scenic reproduction of the war would have shocked all those good people; just as this impossible theatrical deformation, this potpourri of songs, dances and orchestral tremolos charmed and delighted their care-saturated souls.

Little girls in Alsatian costume, and the eternally sublime Red Cross nurse played upon their sentimentality; the slacker inspired them with disgust; they shrieked with delight at the *nouveau riche;* and their enthusiasm knew no bounds when towards eleven-fifteen arrived the "Stars and Stripes" accompanied by a double sextette of khaki-coloured female ambulance drivers. Tradition has willed it thus.

If the war continue any length of time doubtless the United States will also become infuriated with the slacker, and I tremble to think of the special brand of justice that woman in particular will have in store for the man who does not really go to the front, or who, thanks to intrigue and a uniform, is spending his days in peace and safety.

Alas, there are *embusqués* in all countries, just as there are *nouveaux-riches.* In Paris these latter are easily discernible. They have not yet had time to become accustomed to their new luxuries; especially the women, who wear

DOOR OF MADAME HUARD'S HOME——PARIS

exaggerated styles, and flaunt their furs and jewels, which deceive no one.

"They buy everything, so long as it is expensive," explained an antiquity dealer. "They want everything, and want it at once!"

The few old artisans still to be found who are versed in the art of repairing antiques, are rushed to death, and their ill humour is almost comic, for in spite of the fact that they are being well paid for their work, they cannot bear to see these precious treasures falling into the hands of the vulgar.

"This is for Mr. or Mrs. So-and-So," they inform you with an ironical smile, quite certain that you have never heard the name before.

It would almost seem as if a vast wave of prosperity had enveloped the country, were one to judge of the stories of millions made in a minute, fortunes sprung up over night, new factories erected where work never ceases; prices paid for real estate, monster strokes on the Bourse. Little wonder then that in May just past, with the Germans scarcely sixty miles from Paris, the sale of Degas' studio attained the extraordinary total of nearly two million dollars; an Ingres drawing which in

[103]

1889 brought eight hundred and fifty francs, selling for fourteen thousand, and a Greco portrait for which Degas himself gave four hundred and twenty francs in 1894, fetching eighty-two thousand francs.

Yes, such things happen even in France, and one hears but too often of fortunes accumulated in the past four years—but alas! how much more numerous are those which have been lost. The *nouveaux-pauvres* far outnumber the *nouveaux-riches;* but these former seem to go into hiding.

The Parisian bourgeois was essentially a property owner. His delight was in houses; the stone-front six-story kind, the serious rent-paying proposition, containing ten or a dozen moderate-priced apartments, and two good stores, from which he derived a comfortable income. Such was the ultimate desire of the little shop-keeper, desire which spurred him on to sell and to economise.

A house, some French rentes, government bonds (chiefly Russian in recent years) and a few city obligations, were the extent of his investments, and formed not only the nucleus but the better part of many a French fortune.

Imagine then the predicament of such people under the moratorium. Few and far between are the tenants who have paid a sou of rent since August, 1914, and the landlord has no power to collect. Add to this the ever increasing price of living, and you will understand why many an elderly Parisian who counted on spending his declining years in peace and plenty, is now hard at work earning his daily bread.

Made in a moment of emergency, evidently with the intention that it be of short duration, this law about rentals has become the most perplexing question in the world. Several attempts have been made towards a solution, but all have remained fruitless, unsanctioned; and the property owners are becoming anxious.

That men who have been mobilised shall not pay—that goes without saying. But the others. How about them?

I happen to know a certain house in a bourgeois quarter of the city about which I have very special reasons for being well informed.

Both stores are closed. The one was occupied by a book-seller, the other by a bootmaker. Each dealer was called to the army, and both of them have been killed. Their estates will not be settled until after the war.

The first floor was rented to a middle-aged couple. The husband, professor in a city school, is now prisoner in Germany. His wife died during the Winter just passed.

On the second landing one entered the home of a cashier in a big National Bank. He was the proud possessor of a wife and three pretty babies. The husband, aged thirty-two, left for the front with the rank of Lieutenant, the first day of the mobilisation. His bank kindly consented to continue half salary during the war. The lieutenant was killed at Verdun. His employers offered a year and a half's pay to the young widow—that is to say, about six thousand dollars, which she immediately invested in five per cent government rentes. A lieutenant's yearly pension amounts to about three hundred dollars, and the Legion of Honour brings in fifty dollars per annum.

They had scarcely had time to put anything aside, and I doubt if he carried a life insurance. At any rate the education of these little boys will take something more than can be economised after the bare necessities of life have been provided. So how is the brave little woman even to think of paying four years' rent, which when computed would involve more than two-thirds of her capital?

The third floor tenant is an elderly lady who let herself be persuaded to put her entire income into bonds of the City of Vienna, Turkish debt, Russian roubles, and the like. I found her stewing up old newspapers in a greasy liquid, preparing thus a kind of briquette, the only means of heating which she could afford. Yet the prospect of a Winter without coal, possibly without bread, did not prevent her from welcoming me with a smile, and explaining her case with grace and distinction, which denoted the most exquisite breeding. Her maid, she apologised as she bowed me out, was ill of rheumatism contracted during the preceding Winter.

The top apartment was occupied by a government functionary and his family. As captain in the infantry he has been at the front since the very beginning. His wife's family are from Lille, and like most pre-nuptial arrangements when the father is in business, the daughter received but the income of her dowry, which joined to her husband's salary permitted a cheerful, pleasant home, and the prospect of an excellent education for the children.

The salary ceased with the Captain's departure to the front; the wife's income stopped when the Germans entered Lille a few weeks later. They now have but his officer's pay, approximately eighty dollars per month, as entire financial resource. Add to this the death of a mother and four splendid brothers, the constant menace of becoming a widow, and I feel certain that the case will give food for reflection.

All these unfortunate women know each other; have guessed their mutual misfortunes, though, of course, they never mention them. Gathered about a single open fire-place whose welcome blaze is the result of their united economy, they patiently ply their needles at whatever handiwork they are most deft, beading bags, making filet and mesh laces, needle-work tapestry and the like, utilising every spare moment, in the hope of adding another slice of bread to the already too frugal meals.

But orders are rare, and openings for such work almost nil. To obtain a market would demand business training which has not been part of their tradition, which while it tempts, both intimidates and revolts them. Certain desperate ones would branch out in spite of all —but they do not know how, dare not seem so bold.

And so Winter will come anew—Winter with bread and sugar rations at a maximum, Winter with meat prices soaring far above their humble pocket books.

Soup and vegetable stews quickly become the main article of diet. Each succeeding year the little mothers have grown paler, and more frail. The children have lost their fat, rosy cheeks. But let even a local success crown our arms, let the *communiqué* bring a little bit of real news, tell of fresh laurels won, let even the faintest ray of hope for the great final triumph pierce this veil of anxiety—and every heart beat quickens, the smiles burst forth; lips tremble with emotion. These people know the price, and the privilege of being French, the glory of belonging to that holy nation.

V

WHEN after a lengthy search our friends finally discover our Parisian residence, one of the first questions they put is, "Why on earth is your street so narrow?"

The reason is very simple. Merely because la rue Geoffroy L'Asnier was built before carriages were invented, the man who gave it its name having doubtless dwelt there during the fourteenth or fifteenth century, as one could easily infer after inspecting the choir of our parish church. But last Good Friday, the Germans in trying out their super-cannon, bombarded St. Gervais. The roof caved in, killing and wounding many innocent persons, and completely destroying that choir.

Elsewhere a panic might have ensued, but residents of our quarter are not so easily disturbed. The older persons distinctly recall the burning of the Hotel de Ville and the Archbishop's Palace in 1870. And did they not witness the battles in the streets, all the horrors of

[110]

the Commune, after having experienced the agonies and privations of the Siege? I have no doubt that among them there are persons who were actually reduced to eating rats, and I feel quite certain that many a man used his gun to advantage from between the shutters of his own front window.

Their fathers had seen the barricades of 1848 and 1830, their grandfathers before them the Reign of Terror—and so on one might continue as far back as the Norman invasion.

The little café on the rue du Pont Louis-Philippe serves as meeting place for all the prophets and strategists of the quarter, who have no words sufficient to express their disdain for the Kaiser's heavy artillery.

"It's all bluff, they think they can frighten us! Why, I, Madame, I who am speaking to you—I saw the Hotel de Ville, the Theatre des Nations, the grain elevators, all in flames and all at once, the whole city seemed to be ablaze. Well, do you think that prevented the Parisians from fishing in the Seine, or made this café shut its doors? There was a barricade at either end of this street—the blinds were up and you could hear the bullets patter against them. The insurgents, all covered with powder, would sneak over and get a drink—and when finally their barricade was taken, it was the Republican soldiers who sat in our chairs and drank beer and lemonade! *Their* guns, humph! Let them bark!"

It is at this selfsame café that gather all the important men of our district, much as the American would go to his club. They are serious *bourgeois,* well along in the fifties, just a trifle ridiculous, perhaps on account of their allure and their attire. But should one grow to know them better he would soon realise that most of them are shrewd, hard-working business men, each burdened with an anxiety or a sorrow which he never mentions.

They too love strategy. Armies represented by match safes, dominoes and toothpicks have become an obsession—their weakness. They are thorough Frenchmen and their critical sense must be unbridled. They love their ideas and their systems. They would doubtless not hesitate to advise Foch. Personally, if I were Foch, I should turn a deaf ear. But if I were a timid, vacillating, pessimistic spirit, still in doubt as to the final outcome, I should most

certainly seat myself at a neighbouring table
and listen to their conversation that I might
come away imbued with a little of their patience, abnegation, and absolute confidence.

Nor does the feminine opinion deviate from
this course. I found the same ideas prevalent
in the store of a little woman who sold umbrel-
las. Before the war Madame Coutant had a
very flourishing trade, but now her sales are
few and far between, while her chief occupation is repairing. She is a widow without children, and no immediate relative in the war.
Because of this, at the beginning she was
looked down upon and her situation annoyed
and embarrassed her greatly. But by dint of
search, a most voluminous correspondence, and
perhaps a little bit of intrigue, she finally managed to unearth two very distant cousins, peasant boys from the Cevennes, whom she frankly
admitted never having seen, but to whom she
regularly sent packages and post cards; about
whom she was at liberty to speak without
blushing, since one of them had recently been
cited for bravery and decorated with the *Croix
de Guerre*.

This good woman devotes all the leisure and

energy her trade leaves her, to current events. Of course, there is the official *communiqué* which may well be considered as the national health bulletin; but besides that, there is still another, quite as indispensable and fully as interesting, made up of the criticism of local happenings, and popular presumption.

This second *communiqué* comes to us direct from Madame Coutant's, where a triumvirate composed of the scissors-grinder, the woman-who-rents-chairs-in-St.-Gervais, the sacristan's wife, the concierge of the Girls' School, and the widow of an office boy in the City Hall, get their heads together and dispense the news.

The concierges and cooks while out marketing, pick it up and start it on its rounds.

"We are progressing North of the Marne"; "Two million Americans have landed in France," and similar statements shall be accepted only when elucidated, enlarged and embellished by Madame Coutant's group. Each morning brings a fresh harvest of happenings, but each event is certified or contradicted by a statement from some one who is "Out there," and sees and knows.

Under such circumstances an attack in

[114]

Champagne may be viewed from a very different angle when one hears that Bultot, the electrician, is telephone operator in that region; that the aforesaid Bultot has written to his wife in most ambiguous phraseology, and that she has brought the letter to Madame Coutant's for interpretation.

But it is more especially the local moral standards which play an important part and are subject to censorship in Madame Coutant's circle. The individual conduct of the entire quarter is under the most rigid observation. Lives must be pure as crystal, homes of glass. It were better to attempt to hide nothing.

That Monsieur L., the retired druggist, is in sad financial straits, there is not the slightest doubt; no one is duped by the fact that he is trying to put on a bold face under cover of war-time economy.

That the grocer walks with a stick and drags his leg on the ground to make people think he is only fit for the auxiliary service, deceives no one; his time will come, there is but to wait.

Let a woman appear with an unaccustomed furbelow, or a family of a workman that is earning a fat salary, eat two succulent dishes the same week, public opinion will quickly make evident its sentiments, and swiftly put things to rights.

The war must be won, and each one must play his part—do his bit, no matter how humble. The straight and narrow paths of virtue have been prescribed and there is no better guide than the fear of mutual criticism. That is one reason why personally I have never sought to ignore Madame Coutant's opinion.

It goes without saying that the good soul has attributed the participation of the United States in this war entirely to my efforts. And the nature of the advice that I am supposed to have given President Wilson would make an everlasting fortune for a humourist. But in spite of it all, I am proud to belong to them; proud of being an old resident in their quarter.

"Strictly serious people," was the opinion passed upon us by the sacristan's wife for the edification of my new housemaid.

It is a most interesting population to examine in detail, made up of honest, skilful Parisian artisans, *frondeurs* at heart, jesting with everything, but terribly ticklish on the point of honour.

[116]

"They ask us to 'hold out'," exclaims the laundress of the rue de Jouy; "as if we'd ever done anything else all our lives!"

These people were capable of the prodigious. They have achieved the miraculous!

With the father gone to the front, his pay-roll evaporated, it was a case of stop and think. Of course, there was the "Separation fee," about twenty-five cents a day for the mother, ten cents for each child. The French private received but thirty cents *a month* at the beginning of the war. The outlook was anything but cheerful, the possibility of making ends meet more than doubtful. So work it was —or rather, extra work. Eyes were turned towards the army as a means of livelihood. With so many millions mobilised, the necessity for shirts, underwear, uniforms, etc., became evident.

Three or four mothers grouped together and made application for three or four hundred shirts. The mornings were consecrated to house work, which must be done in spite of all, the children kept clean and the food well prepared. But from one o'clock until midnight much might be accomplished; and much was.

The ordinary budget for a woman of the working class consists in earning sufficient to feed, clothe, light and heat the family, besides supplying the soldier husband with tobacco and a monthly parcel of goodies. Even the children have felt the call, and after school, which lasts from eight until four, little girls whose legs must ache from dangling, sit patiently on chairs removing bastings, or sewing on buttons, while their equally tiny brothers run errands, or watch to see that the soup does not boil over.

Then when all is done, when with all one's heart one has laboured and paid everything and there remains just enough to send a money-order to the *poilu,* there is still a happiness held in reserve—a delight as keen as any one can feel in such times; i.e., the joy of knowing that the "Separation fee" has not been touched. It is a really and truly income; it is a dividend as sound as is the State! It has almost become a recompense.

What matter now the tears, the mortal anx-

VIEW OF ST. GERVAIS FROM MADAME
HUARD'S PARIS HOME
(BOMBARDED BY GERMAN SUPER
CANNON, APRIL, 1918)

ieties that it may have cost? For once again, to quote the laundress of the rue de Jouy—

"Trials? Why, we'd have had them anyway, even if there hadn't been a war!"

In these times of strictest economy, it would perhaps be interesting to go deeper into the ways of those untiring thrifty ants who seem to know how "To cut a centime in four" and extract the quintessence from a bone. My concierge is a precious example for such a study, having discovered a way of bleaching clothes without boiling, and numerous recipes for reducing the high cost of living to almost nothing.

It was in her lodge that I was first introduced to a drink made from ash leaves, and then tasted another produced by mixing hops and violets, both to me being equally as palatable as certain brands of grape juice.

Butter, that unspeakable luxury, she had replaced by a savoury mixture of tried out fats from pork and beef kidney, seasoned with salt, pepper, allspice, thyme and laurel, into which at cooling was stirred a glass of milk. Not particularly palatable on bread but as a seasoning to vegetable soup, that mighty

[119]

French stand-by, I found it most excellent.
Believe me, I've tried it!

Jam has long been prepared with honey, and
for all other sweetening purposes she used a
syrup of figs that was not in the least disagree-
able. The ration of one pound of sugar per
person a month, and brown sugar at that, does
not go very far.

The cold season is the chief preoccupation of
all Parisians, and until one has spent a war
winter in the capital he is incapable of realising what can be expected from a scuttle full of
coal.

First of all, one commences by burning it
for heating purposes, rejoicing in every second
of its warmth and glow. One invites one's
friends to such a gala! Naturally the coal
dust has been left at the bottom of the recipient,
the sack in which it was delivered is well shaken
for stray bits, and this together with the sift-
ings is mixed with potter's clay and sawdust,
which latter has become a most appreciable
possession in our day. The whole is then
stirred together and made into bricks or balls,
which though they burn slowly, burn surely.

The residue of this combustible is still so

precious, that when gathered up, ground anew with paper and sawdust, and at length amalgamated with a mucilaginous water composed of soaked flax-seed, one finally obtains a kind of pulp that one tries vainly to make ignite, but which obstinately refuses to do so, though examples to the contrary have been heard of.

The fireless cooker has opened new horizons, for, of course, there is still enough gas to start the heating. But none but the wealthy can afford such extravagance, so each one has invented his own model. My concierge's husband is renowned for his ingenuity in this particular branch, and people from the other side of the Isle St. Louis, or the rue St. Antoine take the time to come and ask his advice. It seems to me he can make fireless cookers out of almost anything. Antiquated wood chests, hat boxes, and even top hats themselves have been utilised in his constructions.

"These are real savings-banks for heat"—he explains pompously—for he loves to tackle the difficult—even adjectively. His shiny bald pate is scarce covered by a Belgian fatigue cap, whose tassel bobs in the old man's eyes, and when he carried his long treasured gold to the

bank, he refused to take its equivalent in notes.
It was necessary to have recourse to the principal cashier, who assured him that if France
needed money she would call upon him first.
Then and then only would he consent to accept.

He is a Lorrainer—a true Frenchman, who
in the midst of all the sorrows brought on by
the conflict, has known two real joys: the first
when his son was promoted and made lieutenant on the battle field; the second when his
friends the Vidalenc and the Lemots made up a
quarrel that had lasted over twelve years.

"I was in a very embarrassing position," he
explained, "for I held both families in equal
esteem. Fortunately the war came and settled
matters. When I say fortunately, of course,
you understand, Madame, what I mean. *'A
quelquechose malheur est bon.'*"

And in truth the original cause of difference
between the Lemots, drapers, and the Vidalenc,
coal and wood dealers, had been lost in the
depths of time. But no hate between Mon-
tague and Capulet was ever more bitter. The
gentle flame of antipathy was constantly kept
kindled by a glance in passing, a half audible
sneer, and if the Vidalenc chose the day of the

White Sale to hang out and beat their stock of coal sacks, one might be certain that the Lemots would be seized with a fit of cleanliness on the coldest of winter days, and would play the hose up and down the street in the freezing air about an hour or so before the Vidalencs would have to unload their coal wagons.

The younger generation, on leaving school every afternoon, would also see to it that the family feud be properly recognised, and many and bitter were the mutual pummelings.

Reconciliation seemed an impossibility, and yet both were hardworking, honest families, economical and gracious, rejoicing in the friendship of the entire quarter, who, of course, were much pained by the situation.

Even the mobilisation failed to bring a truce and the unforgettable words of "Sacred Unity" fell upon arid ground.

But how strange, mysterious and far reaching are the designs of Providence. Young Vidalenc was put into a regiment that was brigaded with the one to which belonged Monsieur Lemot.

The two men met "Out there," and literally fell into each other's arms.

A letter containing a description of this event arrived in the two shops at almost the same moment. That is to say the postman first went to Father Vidalenc's, but by the time the old man had found his spectacles, Madame Lemot had received her missive, and both were practically read at once. Then came the dash for the other's shop, the paper waving wildly in the air.

Of course, they met in the street, stopped short, hesitated, collapsed, wept and embraced, to the utter amazement of the entire quarter who feared not only that something fatal had happened, but also for their mental safety.

Later in the day the news got abroad, and by nightfall every one had heard that Father Vidalenc had washed Madame Lemot's store windows, and that Madame Lemot had promised to have an eye to Vidalenc's accounts, which had been somewhat abandoned since the departure of his son.

When Lemot returned on furlough there was a grand dinner given in his honour at Vidalenc's, and when Vidalenc dined at Lemot's, it was assuredly amusing to see the latter's children all togged out in their Sunday best, a tri-colour bouquet in hand, waiting on their doorstep to greet and conduct the old man.

Unfortunately there was no daughter to give in matrimony so that they might marry and live happily ever after. But on my last trip home I caught a glimpse of an unknown girlish face behind Madame Lemot's counter, and somebody told me it was her niece.

It would not only be unfair, but a gross error on my part to attempt to depict life in our quarter without mentioning one of the most notable inhabitants—namely Monsieur Alexandre Clouet, taylor, so read the sign over the door of the shop belonging to this pompous little person—who closed that shop on August 2nd, 1914, and rallied to the colours. But unlike the vulgar herd he did not scribble in huge chalk letters all over the blinds—"The boss has joined the army." No, indeed, not he!

Twenty four hours later appeared a most elaborate meticulous sign which announced:

MONSIEUR CLOUET.

wishes to inform his numerous customers that he has joined the ranks

[125]

of the 169th infantry, and shall do his duty as a Frenchman.

His wife returned to her father's home, and it was she who pasted up the series of neat little bulletins. First we read:

MONSIEUR CLOUET

is in the trenches but his health is excellent.

He begs his customers and friends to send him news of themselves. Postal Sector 24X.

I showed the little sign to my friends who grew to take an interest in Monsieur Clouet's personal welfare, and passing by his shop they would copy down the latest news and forward it to me, first at Villiers, and afterwards to the States.

It is thus that I learned that Monsieur Clouet, gloriously wounded, had been cared for at a hospital in Cahors, and later on that he had recovered, rejoined his depot and finally returned to the front.

One of my first outings during my last trip sent me in the direction of Monsieur Clouet's abode. I was decidedly anxious to know what had become of him. To my surprise I found the shop open, but a huge announcement hung just above the entrance.

MONSIEUR CLOUET

gloriously wounded and decorated with the Military Medal, regrets to state that in future it will be impossible for him to continue giving his personal attention to his business.

His wife and his father-in-law will hereafter combine their efforts to give every satisfaction to his numerous customers.

I entered. For the moment the wife and the father-in-law were combining their efforts to convince a very stout, elderly gentleman that check trousers would make him look like a sylph.

"Ah, Madame, what a surprise," she cried, on seeing me.

"But your husband?" I queried. "Is it really serious—do tell me!"

"Alas, Madame, he says he'll never put his foot in the shop again. You see he's very sensitive since he was scalped, and he's afraid somebody might know he has to wear a wig!"

VI

THE Boche aeroplane was by no means a
novelty to the Parisian. Its first apparitions
over the capital (1914) were greeted with curious enthusiasm, and those who did not have a
field glass handy at the time, later on satisfied
their curiosity by a visit to the Invalides, where
every known type of enemy machine was displayed in the broad court-yard.

The first Zeppelin raid (April 15th, 1915)
happened toward midnight, and resulted in
a good many casualties, due not to the bombs
dropped by the enemy, but to the number of
colds and cases of pneumonia and bronchitis
caught by the pajama-clad Parisian, who
rushed out half covered, to see the sight,
thoughtlessly banging his front door behind
him.

But the first time that we were really driven
to take shelter in the cellar was after dinner at
the home of a friend who lives in an apartment
house near the Avenue du Bois. We were en-

joying an impromptu concert of chamber music, when the alarm was given, swiftly followed by distant but very distinct detonations, which made hesitation become imprudence.

The descent to the basement was accomplished without undue haste, or extraordinary commotion, save for an old Portuguese lady and her daughter who lost their heads and unconsciously gave us a comic interlude, worthy of any first-class movie.

Roused from her sleep, the younger woman with self preservation uppermost in her mind, had slipped on an outer garment, grabbed the first thing she laid her hands on, and with hair streaming over her back, dashed down five long flights of stairs.

At the bottom she remembered her mother, let forth an awful shriek, and still holding her bottle of tooth wash in her hands, jumped into the lift and started in search of her parent.

In the meantime, the latter on finding her daughter's bed empty, had started towards the lower floors, crossing the upward bound lift, which Mademoiselle was unable to stop.

Screams of terror, excited sentences in Portuguese—in which both gave directions that neither followed, and for a full ten minutes mother and daughter raced up and down in the lift and on the stairway, trying vainly to join one another.

A young lieutenant home on leave, at length took pity on them and finally united the two exhausted creatures who fell into each other's arms shrieking hysterically:

"If we must die—let us die together!"

The concierges and the servants began arranging chairs and camp stools around the furnace; the different tenants introduced themselves and their guests. Almost every one was still about when the signal was given, and this cellar where the electric lamps burned brightly soon took on the aspect of a drawing-room, in spite of all. One lone man, however, stood disconsolate, literally suffocating beneath a huge cavalry cape, hooked tight up to his throat. As the perspiration soon began rolling from his forehead, a friend seeking to put him at his ease, suggested he open up his cloak.

The gentleman addressed cast a glance over the assembled group, broadened out into a smile, and exclaimed—

[130]

"I can't. Only got my night shirt underneath."

The hilarity was general, and the conversation presently became bright and sparkling with humorous anecdotes.

The officers held their audience spellbound with fear and admiration; the women talked hospital and dress, dress and hospital, finally jesting about the latest restrictions. One lady told the story of a friend who engaged a maid, on her looks and without a reference, the which maid shortly became a menace because of her propensity for dropping and breaking china.

One day, drawn towards the pantry by the sound of a noise more terrible than any yet experienced, she found the girl staring at a whole pile of plates—ten or a dozen—which had slipped from her fingers and lay in thousands of pieces on the floor.

The lady became indignant and scolded.

"Ah, if Madame were at the front, she'd see worse than that!" was the consoling response.

"But we're not at the front, I'll have you understand, and what's more neither you nor I have ever been there, my girl."

"I beg Madame's pardon, but my last place

[131]

was in a hospital at Verdun, as Madame will see when my papers arrive."

General laughter was cut short by the sound of two explosions.

"They're here. They've arrived. It will soon be over now," and like commentaries were added.

A servant popped the cork of a champagne bottle, and another passed cakes and candied fruit.

An elderly man who wore a decoration, approached the officers.

"Gentlemen," said he, "excuse me for interrupting, but do any of you know the exact depth to which an aeroplane bomb can penetrate?"

The officers gave him a few details, which, however, did not seem to satisfy the old fellow. His anxiety became more and more visible.

"I wouldn't worry, sir, if I were you. There's absolutely no danger down here."

"Thank you for your assurance, Messieurs," said he, "but I'm not in the least anxious about my personal safety. It's my drawings and my collection of porcelains that are causing me such concern. I thought once that I'd box

[132]

them all up and bring them down here. But you never can tell what dampness or change of temperature might do to a water colour or a gouache. Oh! my poor Fragonards! My poor Bouchers! Gentlemen, never, never collect water colours or porcelains! Take it from me!"

At that moment the bugle sounded—"All's well," and as we were preparing to mount the stairs, the old man accosted the officers anew, asking them for the titles of some books on artillery and fortification.

"That all depends to what use you wish to apply them."

"Ah, it's about protecting my collection. I simply must do something! I can't send them to storage, they wouldn't be any safer there, and even if they were I'd die of anxiety so far away from my precious belongings."

"Good-nights" were said in the vestibule, and the gathering dispersed just as does any group of persons after a theatre or an ordinary reception. But once in the street, it was absolutely useless to even think of a taxi. People were pouring from every doorway, heads stuck out of every window.

"Where did they fall? Which way?"

In the total obscurity, the sound of feet all hurrying in the same direction, accompanied by shouts of recognition, even ripples of laughter, seemed strangely gruesome, as the caravan of curious hastened towards the scene of tragedy.

"No crowds allowed. Step lively," called the *sergeants-de-ville,* at their wits' end. "Better go back home, they might return. Step lively, I say!"

It happened thus the first few visits, but presently the situation became less humorous. One began to get accustomed to it. Then one commenced to dislike it and protest.

Seated by the studio fire, we were both plunged deep in our books.

"Allons!" exclaimed H. "Do you hear the *pompiers?* The Gothas again!"

We stiffened up in our chairs and listened. The trumpets sounded shrilly on the night air of our tranquil Parisian quarter.

"Right you are. That means down we go! They might have waited until I finished my chapter, hang them! There's no electricity in our cellar," and I cast aside my book in disgust.

Taking our coats and a steamer rug we prepared to descend. In the court-yard the clatter of feet resounded.

The cellar of our seventeenth century dwelling being extremely deep and solidly built, was at once commandeered as refuge for one hundred persons in case of bombardment, and we must needs share it with some ninety odd less fortunate neighbours.

"Hurry up there. Hurry up, I say," calls a sharp nasal voice.

That voice belonged to Monsieur Leddin, formerly a clock maker, but now of the *Service Auxiliare,* and on whom devolved the policing of our entire little group, simply because of his uniform.

His observations, however, have but little effect. People come straggling along, yawning from having been awakened in their first sleep, and almost all of them is hugging a bundle or parcel containing his most precious belongings.

It is invariably an explosion which finally

livens their gait, and they hurry into the stairway. A slight jam is thus produced.

"No pushing there! Order!" cries another stentorian voice, belonging to Monsieur Vidalenc, the coal dealer.

"Here! here!" echo several high pitched trebles. *"Très bien, très bien.* Follow in line —what's the use of crowding?"

Monsieur Leddin makes another and still shriller effort, calling from above:

"Be calm now. Don't get excited."

"Who's excited?"

"You are!"

"Monsieur Leddin, you're about as fit to be a soldier as I to be an Archbishop," sneered the butcher's wife. "You'd do better to leave us alone and hold your peace."

General hilarity, followed by murmurs of approval from various other females, which completely silenced Monsieur Leddin, who never reopened his mouth during the entire evening, so that one could not tell whether he was nursing his offended dignity or hiding his absolute incompetence to assume authority.

Places were quickly found on two or three long wooden benches, and a few chairs provided for the purpose, some persons even spreading out blankets and camping on the floor.

The raiment displayed was the typical negligée of the Parisian working class; a dark coloured woollen dressing gown, covered over with a shawl or a cape, all the attire showing evidence of having been hastily donned with no time to think of looking in the mirror.

An old lantern and a kerosene lamp but dimly lighted the groups which were shrouded in deep velvety shadows.

Presently a man, a man that I had never seen before, a man with a long emaciated face and dark pointed beard, rose in the background, holding a blanket draped about him by flattening his thin white hand against his breast. The whole scene seemed almost biblical, and instantly my mind evoked Rembrandt's masterpiece—the etching called 'The Hundred Florin Piece,' which depicts the crowds seated about the standing figure of our Saviour and listening to His divine words.

But the spell was quickly broken when an instant later my vision coughed and called—

"Josephine, did you bring down the 'Petit Parisien,' as I told you?"

Ten or fifteen minutes elapsed, and then a rather distant explosion gave us reason to believe that the enemy planes were retiring.

"*Jamais de la vie!* No such luck to-night. Why we've got a good couple of hours ahead of us, just like last time. You'll see! Much better to make yourself as comfortable as possible and not lose any sleep over it."

The tiny babies had scarcely waked at all, and peacefully continued to slumber on their mothers' knees, or on improvised cots made from a blanket or comforter folded to several thicknesses.

The women soon yawned, and leaning their backs against the wall nodded regularly in spite of their efforts not to doze off, and each time, surprised by the sudden shock of awakening would shudder and groan unconsciously.

Tightly clasped in their hands, or on the floor between their feet lay a bag which never got beyond their reach, to which they clung as something sacred. Certain among them were almost elegant in their grey linen covers. Others had seen better days, while still others dated back to the good old times of needlework tapestry. There were carpet, kit and canvas bags, little wooden chests with leather handles, and one poor old creature carefully harboured a card-board box tied about with a much knotted string.

What did they all contain? In France amid such a gathering it were safe to make a guess.

First of all, the spotless family papers— cherished documents registering births, deaths and marriages. A lock of hair, a baby tooth, innumerable faded photographs, a bundle of letters, a scrap of paper whereon are scrawled the last words of a departed hero, and way down underneath, neatly separated from all the rest, I feel quite sure the little family treasure lies hidden. Yes, here is that hand- ful of stocks and bonds, thanks to which their concierge bows to them with respect; those earnings that permit one to fall ill, to face old age and death without apprehension, the assur- ance the children shall want for nothing, shall have a proper education—the certitude that the two little rooms occupied can really be called home; that the furniture so carefully waxed and polished is one's own forever. Bah! what

terrors can lack of work, food shortage, or war
hold for such people? Thus armed can they
not look the horrid spectres square in the
face? The worst will cost but one or two blue
bank notes borrowed from the little pile, but
because of the comfort they have brought they
will be replaced all the more gayly when better days shall come.

All this ran through my brain as I watched
those hands—big and small, fat and thin,
young and old, clasping their treasure so
tightly, and I couldn't help feeling that gigantic convulsive gesture of thousands of other
women, who all over the great Capital at that
same moment were hugging so lovingly their
little all; the fruit of so much toil and so much
virtue.

My reflections were cut short by a deafening
noise that roused my sleeping companions.
The children shrieked, and the women openly
lamented.

"That was a close call," commented Monsieur Neu, our concierge.

Five or six boys wanted to rush out and
see where the bomb had fallen. They were dis-
suaded, but with difficulty.

An elderly man had taken his six year old grandson on to his knee, and that sleepy little Parisian urchin actually clapped his hands and crowed over the shock.

"Jiminy, that was a fine one!"

"That's right, my child," pompously exclaimed the grandsire. "Never, never forget the monsters who troubled your innocent sleep with their infamous crimes."

"Oh, cut it out, grandpop," was the somewhat irreverent reply. "Aren't you afraid you might miss forty winks?" and then turning to his mother, "I say, mamma, if one of them lands on our house, you promise you'll wake me up, won't you? I want to see everything, and last time and the time before, I missed it!"

"Yes, darling, of course, but go to sleep, there's a good boy."

A tall, good-looking girl over in one corner openly gave vent to her sentiments.

"The idiots! the idiots! if they think they can scare us that way! They'd far better not waste their time, and let us sleep. It isn't a bit funny any more, and I've got to work just the same to-morrow, Boche or no Boche!"

Two rickety old creatures clasped each other in arms, and demanded in trembling voices if there was any real danger! This produced a ripple of merriment.

Monsieur Duplan, the butcher, then asked the ladies' permission to smoke, the which permission was graciously accorded.

"Why, if I'd only thought, I'd have brought down another lamp and my work. It's too bad to waste so much time."

"I have my knitting. You don't need any light for that."

"Where on earth did you get wool? How lucky you are!"

From Monsieur Leddin's lips now rose a loud and sonorous snore.

"Decidedly that man is possessed of all the charms," giggled a sarcastic neighbour.

"Yes, it must be a perfect paradise to live with such an angel, and to feel that you've got him safe at home till the end of the war. I don't wonder his poor little wife took the children and went to Burgundy."

"Why isn't he at the front?" hissed some one in a whisper.

"Yes—why?"

"There are lots less healthy men than he out there. The fat old plumber who lived on the rue de Jouy, and who can hardly breathe, was taken——"

"And the milkman who passed a hundred and three medical inspections and finally had to go."

"If you think my husband is overstrong, you're mistaken."

"And mine, Madame, how about him?"

Something told me that Monsieur Leddin's fate was hanging in the balance on this eventful evening.

"Shake him up, Monsieur Neu, he doesn't need to sleep if we can't. We've all got to work to-morrow and he can take a nice long nap at his desk."

"Oh, leave him alone," put in Monsieur Laurent, the stationer, who was seated near me. "Just listen to those fiendish women. Why they're worse than we are about the slackers. After all, I keep telling them there must be a few, otherwise who's going to write history? And history's got to be written, hasn't it?"

"Most decidedly," I replied.

And having at length found a subject of

conversation that I had deigned approve, he continued,

"Just think of what all the poor kids in generations to come will have to cram into their heads! The names of all the battles on all the Fronts and the dates. It makes me dizzy! I'm glad it's not up to me. I like history all well enough, but I'd rather make it than have to learn it."

Monsieur Laurent did not speak lightly. He had veritably helped to make history, having left his right foot and part of his leg "Out there" on the hills of Verdun.

I asked him how he was getting along since his return.

"Better than ever! Excellent appetite—never a cold—never an ill. I'll soon be as spry as a rabbit. Why, I used to be too heavy, I always fell asleep after luncheon. That campaign set my blood to rights. I'm ten years younger," he exclaimed, pounding his chest.

"That's a good strong-box, isn't it?" and he coughed loudly to thoroughly convince of its solidity.

"France can still count on me! I was ready for war, and I shall be prepared for peace."

[144]

THE COURTYARD LEADING TO
MADAME HUARD'S CELLAR

"Just wait till it gets here," murmured some woman.

"It'll come, it's bound to come some time," he cried, evidently pursuing a favourite theme. "And we'll like it all the better for having waited so long."

Monsieur Laurent has firm faith in the immediate business future.

"*Voilà!* all we've got to do is to lay Germany out flat. Even then the economical struggle that will follow the war will be terrible," he prophesies. "The French must come to the fore with all the resources of their national genius. As to myself, I have my own idea on the subject."

We were fairly drinking in his words.

"You've all doubtless seen the sign that I put up in my window?"

We acquiesced.

"Well, it was that sign that opened my eyes."

I was all attention by this time, for I distinctly remembered the above mentioned sign. It had puzzled and amused me immensely. Painted in brilliant letters, it ran as follows:

EXCEPTIONAL BARGAIN:

For men having their left foot ampu-
tated and wearing size No. 9.
3 shoes for the right foot—two
black and one tan; excellent
quality, almost like new.
For sale, or exchange for shoes be-
longing to the left foot. Must be
of same quality and in like condition.

"I haven't yet made any special effort to ascertain whether there are more amputations of the left than of the right foot," continued Monsieur Laurent; "I suppose it's about equal. Well, my plan is just this. As soon as there's peace I'm going to set up shop on the rue St. Antoine, or the Place de la Bastille. I'll call it 'A la botte de l'amputé,' and I sell my shoes separately instead of in pairs. There's a fortune in it inside of five years."

"Just hear him raving," sighed his wife. "You know well enough, Laurent, that just so soon as the war is over we're going to sell out, and with the money, your pension, and what we've saved up, we'll go out to the Parc St. Maur, buy a little cottage and settle down. I'll

[146]

raise a few chickens and some flowers, and you can go fishing in the Seine all day long."

"But the economical struggle?"

"You let the economical struggle take care of itself. Now, with your mad idea, just suppose those who had a right foot all wanted tan shoes, and those who had a left couldn't stand anything but black? I'd like to know where you'd be then? Stranger things than that have happened."

Laurent gazed at his wife in admiration.

"With all your talk about the future, it seems to me we've been down here a long time since that last explosion."

One woman looked for her husband but could not find him. The Rembrandt Christhead had also disappeared.

A tall fifteen year old lad who stood near the door informed us that they had slipped out to see.

"So has Germain."

"Then you come here! Don't you dare leave me," scolded the mother. "Can you just see something happening to him with his father out there in the trenches?"

Monsieur Neu and two other men soon followed suit.

The big boy who had so recently been admonished managed to crawl from beneath his mother's gaze and make his escape.

"If ever I catch him, he'll find out what my name is," screamed the excited woman, dashing after him into the darkness.

Then, presently, one by one we took our way towards the hall, and the cellar seemed empty.

The tall boy came back to the entrance, all excitement.

"We saw where it fell!" he panted. "There are some wounded. The police won't let you go near. There's lots and lots of people out there. Where's mamma?"

"She's looking for you!"

He was off with a bound.

The instinct to see, to know what is going on is infinitely stronger than that of self preservation. Many a soldier has told me that, and I have often had occasion to prove it personally.

Some of the women started towards the street.

"We're only going as far as the door," said they by way of excuse. "You're really quite safe beneath the portico." And they carried their babies with them.

So when the final signal of safety was sounded, there remained below but a few old women, a couple of very small children, and Monsieur Leddin, whom nothing seemed to disturb.

The mothers returned to fetch their children. The old ladies and Monsieur Leddin were aroused.

"C'est fini! Ah!"

And in the courtyard one could hear them calling as they dispersed.

"Good-night, Madame Cocard."

"Good-night, Madame Bidon."

"Don't forget."

"I won't."

"Till next time."

"That's it, till next time."

A young woman approached me.

"Madame, you won't mind if I come after them to-morrow, would you?" she begged with big wistful eyes. "The stairway is so dark and so narrow in our house, I'm afraid something might happen to them."

"Mercy me! you're surely not thinking of leaving your babies alone in the cellar?"

"Oh, Madame, it's not my babies. Not yet," and she smiled. "It's my bronze chimney ornaments!"

"Your what?"

"Yes, Madame, my chimney ornaments. A clock and a pair of candlesticks. They're over there in that wooden box all done up beautifully. You see Lucien and I got married after the war began. It was all done so quickly that I didn't have any trousseau or wedding presents. I'm earning quite a good deal now, and I don't want him to think ill of me so I'm furnishing the house, little by little. It's a surprise for when he comes home."

"He's at the front?"

"No, Madame, in the hospital. He has a bad face wound. My, how it worried him. He wanted to die, he used to be so handsome! See, here's his photograph. He isn't too awfully ugly, is he? Anyway I don't love him a bit less; quite the contrary, and that's one of the very reasons why I want to fix things up—so as to prove it to him!"

VII

THE Moulin Rouge no longer turns. The
strains of sounding brass and tinkling cymbal
which once issued incessantly from every
open café, and together with the street
cries, the tram bells and the motor horns of
the Boulevards Extérieurs, formed a gigantic
characteristic medley, have long since died
away. The night restaurants are now turned
into workrooms and popular soup kitchens.
Montmartre, the heart of Paris, as it used to
be called, Montmartre the care-free, has become drawn and wizened as a winter apple,
and at present strangely resembles a little
provincial city.

If it were true that "There is no greater sorrow than recalling happy times when in
misery," doubtless from France would rise but
one long forlorn wail. The stoic Parisian
poilu, however, has completely reversed such
philosophy, and unmindful of the change his
absence has created, delights in the remem-

brance of every instant, dreams but of the moment when he shall again be part of the lighthearted throngs who composed the society of the Butte. Time and again I have seen heavy army trucks lumbering down the avenue, bearing in huge chalk letters on either side of the awning-covered sides, such inscriptions as— *Bon jour, Montmartre. A bientot la Cigale— Greetings from the Front*—and like nonsense, denoting not only a homesick heart, but a delicate attention towards a well beloved.

A few months might have made but little difference, but each succeeding year of war has brought indelible changes. Gone forever, I fear, are the evenings when after dinner at the Cuckoo, we would stand on the balcony and watch the gradual fairy-like illumination of the panorama that stretched out before us. The little restaurant has closed its doors, but the vision from the terrace is perhaps more majestic, for as the last golden rays of twilight disappear, a deep purple vapour rising from the unknown, rolls forward and mysteriously envelops the *Ville Lumière* in its sumptuous protecting folds. Alone, overhead the star lamp of a scout plane is the only visible light.

The old Moulin de la Galette has cast
aside its city airs and taken on a most rural
aspect, while the *maquis,* or jungle on whose
site a whole new white stone quarter had been
projected, is now but a mass of half finished,
abandoned foundations, wherein the children
of the entire neighbourhood gather to play at
the only game which now has a vogue, i.e.,
"War."

La petite guerre they call it.

We came upon them quite by accident one
afternoon, and discovered two hostile bands oc-
cupying first line trenches.

Of course, as no one wished to be the Boche,
it looked for a time as though the campaign
would have to be deferred, but so violent was
the love of fray that it was soon decided that
the *opposite* side in both cases would be considered Hun, and thus the difficulty was solved.

It goes without saying that the school which
is first dismissed occupies the better positions.
The others must rely upon their strength and
valour to win out.

The first attack was with hand grenades in
the form of pebbles. Patrols advanced into
No Man's Land, crawling and crouching until

with a yell the belligerents met. Prisoners were taken on both sides.

"What forces have we in front of us?" demanded an important looking twelve year old General of an enemy soldier who was brought before him.

Dead silence ensued.

"If he refuses to answer, turn him upside down until he does."

The order was executed.

From the opposite trench came shrieks of "Boche! Boche!—it's only the Boche who maltreat prisoners."

The aforementioned who was rapidly developing cerebral congestion, made sign that he would speak.

"Turn him right side up!"

The young executioner obeyed, but still held a firm grip on the unfortunate lad's collar.

"Now, then, how many of you are there in your trenches?"

"Enough to make jelly out of your men if there are many like you!" shrieked the captive, struggling to escape.

"Take him behind the lines, don't be rough with him. Respect is due all prisoners," ordered the General, whose eye had caught a glimpse of his army being menaced by the blond headed enemy.

"Look out, boys! Down with your heads! They're sending over some 'coal scuttles.' Dig in I say and keep a sharp look out! What's the matter back there?"

"It's little Michaud. He's wounded!"

"Don't cry, Michaud, go out by the connecting trench to the dressing station. It's not far."

The hail of "coal scuttles" having subsided, the General mounted to his observation post.

"Hey! Michel! Gaston! hey there, the artillery!" he yelled. "Get in at them quick. Go to it, I say. Don't you see they're going to attack! What's artillery for, anyway?"

"We can't fire a shot. They're pounding on our munitions dump."

"What difference does that make?"

Under heavy fire the artillery achieved the impossible, which actually resulted in bloodshed. But their determination was soon rewarded, for the patent "Seventy Fives," represented by huge slabs of sod, soon rained into the enemy trenches, sowing panic and disorder.

Profiting by the confusion, our General grabbed up a basket and began distributing munitions.

"Attention! Listen to me! Don't any one fire until I give the word. Let them approach quite close and then each one of you choose your man. Dentu, if you're too short, stand on a stone or something!"

The artillery wreaking havoc in his midst, the enemy decided to brusque matters and attack. He left his trenches shouting, *"Vive la France! En avant! Aux armes, mes citoyens! A bas le Boche!"*

"Attention! Are you ready? Fire!" commanded our General.

Bing! bang! a veritable tornado of over-ripe tomatoes deluged the astonished oncomers, who hesitated an instant and then fell back. The standard bearer having received one juicy missile full in the face, dropped his emblem and stared wild-eyed about him. From the head and hair of the enemy General, whose cardboard helmet had been crushed to a pulp, streamed a disgusting reddish mess. The other unfortunate wounded were weeping.

"En avant à la bayonette! Vive la France!

We've got them, they're ours," shrieked the delighted commander, who owed his rank to the
fact that his parents kept a fruit stand.

It was victory for certain, and a proudly won
triumph. The mêlée was hot and ferocious,
many a patch or darn being put in store for
certain patient, all-enduring mothers.

The dressing station was full to overflowing.
Here the feminine element reigned supreme,
their heads eclipsed beneath a stolen dish cloth,
a borrowed towel, or a grimy handkerchief.
And here too, little Michaud, his pate enveloped in so many yards of bandage that he
seemed to be all turban, sat on an impromptu
cot, smiling benignly while devouring a three
sou apple tart, due to the generosity of the
Ladies' Red Cross Emergency Committee,
which had taken up a collection in order to al-
leviate the sufferings of their dear hero.

To be perfectly frank, almost all the supply of dressings had been employed on Michaud's person at the very outbreak of hostilities,
so, therefore, when the stock ran short and
more were needed, they were merely unrolled
from about his head.

Leaving him to his fate, we advanced a bit

in order to communicate with one of the glorious vanquished.

"They think they've got us," he explained, "but just you wait and see! I know a shop on the Avenue de Clichy where you can get rotten eggs for nothing! They don't know what's coming to them—they don't!"

Thus for these little folks the very state of their existence is the war. They do not talk about it because they are living it. Even those who are so fortunate as to recall the happy times when there was no conflict, scarcely assume a superiority over their comrades who cannot remember that far distant epoch.

"My papa'll be home next week on furlough if there isn't an attack," or "Gee, how we laughed down cellar the night of the bombardment," are common phrases, just as the words, "guns, shells, aeroplanes and gas," form the very elements of their education. The better informed instruct the others, and it is no uncommon occurrence to see a group of five or six little fellows hanging around a doorway, listening to a gratuitous lecture on the 75, given by an elder.

"That's not true," cuts in one. "It's not that

at all, the *correcteur* and the *debouchoir* are
not the same thing. Not by a long sight! I
ought to know, hadn't I, my father's chief gunner in his battery."

"Ah, go on! Didn't Mr. Dumont who used
to teach the third grade, draw it all out for us
on the blackboard the last time he was home
on leave? What do you take us for? Why
he's even got the *Croix de Guerre* and the
"Bananna." *

Nor is the *communiqué* ignored by these
budding heroes. On the contrary, it is read
and commented upon with fervour.

In a little side street leading to the Seine, I
encountered a ten year old lad, dashing forward, brandishing the evening paper in his
hand.

"Come on, kids, it's time for the *communiqué*," he called to a couple of smaller boys who
were playing on the opposite curb. The children addressed (one may have been five, the
other seven, or thereabouts) immediately abandoned their marbles, and hastened to join their

* The "Bananna"—slang for the Medaille Militaire
—probably on account of the green and yellow ribbon
on which it hangs.

[159]

companion, who breathlessly unfolded the sheet.

. "Artillery combats in Flanders——" he commenced.

The little fellows opened their big candid eyes, their faces were drawn and grave, in an intense effort of attention. Their mouths gaped unconsciously. One felt their desire to understand, to grasp things that were completely out of reach.

"During the night a spirited attack with hand grenades in the region of the Four de Paris," continued the reader. "We progressed slightly to the East of Mort Homme, and took an element of trenches. We captured two machine guns, and made several prisoners."

"My papa's in Alsace," piped one listener.

. "And mine's in the Somme."

"That's all right," inferred the elder. "Isn't mine at Verdun?" and then proudly, "And machine gunner at that!"

. Then folding his paper and preparing to move on:

"The news is good—we should worry."

Yes, that's what the little ones understood best of all, "the news is good," and a wonder-

[160]

A COURTYARD IN MONTMARTRE

ful, broad, angelic smile spread out over their fresh baby faces; a smile so bewitching that I couldn't resist embracing them—much to their surprise.

"I just must kiss you," I explained, "because the news is good!"

From one end to the other of the entire social scale the children have this self same spirit.

Seated at the dining-room table, a big spot of violet ink on one cheek, I found little Jules Gauthier carefully copying something in a note book.

"What are you doing there, Jules?"

"Writing in my book, Madame."

"What are you writing?"

"About the war, everything I can remember."

At that particular moment he was inscribing an ancedote which he had just heard some one telling in his mother's drawing room.

"The President of the Republic once asked General de Castelnau, 'Well, General, what shall you do after the war is over?'

" 'Weep for my sons, Mr. President.' "

[161]

"But, Jules, why do you write such things?"
I queried.

"Because it's splendid, and I put down
everything I know or hear that's beautiful or
splendid."

And true enough, pêle mêle with portraits
he had cut out and pasted, plans for aeroplanes
that he had drawn, were copies of extraordinary citations for bravery, memorable dates
and descriptions of battles.

In the Summer of 1915, my friend Jeanne
took her small baby and her daughter Annette,
aged five, to their little country home on the
seashore in Brittany. The father, over military
age, remained in town to look after some patriotic work.

Help was hard to get, and Jeanne not over
strong was torn between household duties and
her infant son, so that Annette, clad in a bath-
ing suit and sweater, spent most of her time
on the beach in company with other small
people of her own years.

Astonished at seeing the little one so much
alone, certain kind-hearted mothers invited
her to partake of their bread, chocolate and

other dainties provided for the *gouter* of their own offspring, and as the child gladly and continually accepted, her apparent abandon became a subject of conversation, and they decided to question Annette.

"Where is your mother, dear?"

"She's home, very ill."

"Oh, really. I'm so sorry, what's the trouble—nothing serious, I hope?"

"I think it must be—you see she has had her three brothers killed and now grandpa has enlisted."

"Dear me, how terrible! And your papa?"

"Oh, he's in town working for the government. One of his brothers was killed and the other is blind. Poor old grandma died of the shock."

Moved by the lamentable plight of so young a mother, the good ladies sought to penetrate her seclusion, offer their condolences, and help lift the cloud of gloom.

Imagine then their surprise at being received by my smiling, blond-haired friend, who failed to comprehend their mournful but astonished looks.

At length Annette's story was brought to

[163]

light, and Jeanne could but thank them for
their trouble, at the same time explaining that
neither she nor her husband had ever had
brothers, and that their parents had been dead
these many years.

"You naughty, wicked girl!" scolded
Jeanne, as her tearful progeny was led forward. "You wicked, wicked girl—what made
you tell such lies?"

The culprit twisted her hands; her whole
body fairly convulsed with restrained sobs.

"Answer me at once! Do you hear me?"

Annette hesitated, and then throwing herself in her mother's arms, blurted out, "Oh,
mamma, I just couldn't help it! All the
others were so proud of their *poilus,* and I
haven't any one at the front; not even a god-
son!"

It seems highly probable that children who
have received such an education will ulti-
mately form a special generation. Poor little
things who never knew what "play" meant,
at a time when life should have been all sun-
shine and smiles; tender, sensitive creatures
brought up in an atmosphere of privation and
tears.

Those who were between ten and fifteen years of age at the outbreak of the war have had a particularly hard time.

In the smaller trades and industries, as well as on the farms, with a father or an elder brother absent, these youngsters have been obliged to leave school or college, and hasten to the counter or the plough. And not only have they been called upon to furnish the helping hand, but in times of moral stress they have often had to give proof of a mature judgment, a courage, a will power, and a forebearance far beyond their years.

After a ten months' absence, when I opened up my Parisian home, I found it necessary to change or replace certain electric lighting arrangements. As usual I called up the Maison Bincteux.

"Bien, Madame, I shall send some one to look after it."

The next morning my maid announced *La Maison Bincteux.*

When I reached the hallway, I found the aforesaid *Maison* to be a lad some fifteen years old, who might easily have passed for twelve, so slight was his build. His long, pale, oval face, which seemed almost unhealthy, was relieved by a pair of snapping blue eyes.

"Did you bring a letter?"

"Oh, no, Madame, I am Monsieur Bincteux's son."

"Then your father is coming later?"

"Oh, no, Madame, he can't, he is mechanician in the aviation corps at Verdun. My oldest brother is in the artillery, and the second one has just left for the front—so I quit school and am trying to help mother continue the business."

"How old are you?"

"I belong to the Class of 1923," came the proud reply.

"Oh, I see. Come right in then, I'll show you what I need."

With a most serious and important air he produced a note book, tapped on the partitions, sounded the walls, took measures and jotted down a few lines.

"Very well, Madame, I've seen all that's necessary. I'll be back to-morrow morning with a workman."

True to his word he appeared the next day, accompanied by a decrepit, coughing, asthmatic specimen of humanity, who was hardly worthy of the honorable title his employer had seen fit to confer.

Our studio is extremely high, and when it was necessary to stretch out and raise our double extension ladder, it seemed as though disaster were imminent.

We offered our assistance, but from the glance he launched us, I felt quite certain that we had mortally offended the manager of the *Maison Bincteux*. He stiffened every muscle, gave a supreme effort, and up went the ladder. Truly his will power, his intelligence and his activity were remarkable.

After surveying the undertaking, he made his calculations, and then addressing his aid:

"We'll have to bore here," he said. "The wires will go through there, to the left and we'll put the switches to the right, just above; go ahead with the work and I'll be back in a couple of hours."

The old man mumbled something disobliging.

"Do what I tell you and don't make any fuss about it. You're better off here than in the trenches, aren't you? We've heard enough from you, old slacker."

The idea that any one dare insinuate that he ought to be at the front at his age, fairly suffocated the aid electrician, who broke into a fit of coughing.

"Madame, Madame," he gasped. "In the trenches? Why I'm seventy-three. I've worked for his father and grandfather before him—but I've never seen his like! Why only this very morning he was grumbling because I didn't ride a bicycle so we could get to places faster!"

At noon the *Maison Bincteux* reappeared, accompanied by the General Agent of the Electric Company. He discussed matters in detail with this awe inspiring person—objected, retaliated, and finally terminated his affairs, leaving us a few moments later, having accomplished the best and most rapid job of its kind I have ever seen.

With the Class of 1919 now behind the lines, by the time this volume goes to press, there is little doubt but that the class of 1920 shall have been called to the colours. All these lads are the little fellows we used to know in short trousers; the rascals who not so many summers since climbed to the house-tops, swung from trees, fell into the river, dropped torpedoes to frighten the horses or who when punished and locked in their rooms, would jump out the window and escape.

Then, there were those others, "the good boys," whose collars and socks were always immaculate, romantic little natures that would kiss your hand with so much ceremony and politeness, blushing if one addressed them affectionately, spending whole days at a time lost in fantastic reveries.

To us they hardly seem men. And yet they are already soldiers, prepared to make the supreme sacrifice, well knowing from father, brothers or friends who have gone before, all the grandeur and abnegation through which their souls must pass to attain but an uncertain end.

Any number of what we would call mere children have been so imbued with the spirit of sacrifice, that they have joined the army long before their Class was called. Madame de Martel's grandson, the sons of Monsieur Barthou, Louis Morin, Pierre Mille, to mention but a few in thousands, all fell on the Field of Honour before attaining their eighteenth year.

And each family will tell you the same pathetic tale:

"We tried to interest him in his work—we provided all kinds of amusements; did everything to keep him here; all to no avail. There was just one thought uppermost in his mind—Enlist—Serve. He was all we had!"

Little Jacques Krauss promised his mother he would not go until he had won his baccalaureate, and my friend lived in the hope that all would be over by the time the "baby" had succeeded. But, lo! the baby, unknown to his parents, worked nights, skipped a year, passed his examination, and left for the front, aged seventeen years and three months! He had kept his word. What could they do?

In another household—my friends the G's., where two elder sons have already been killed, there remained as sole heir, a pale, lanky youth of sixteen.

With the news of his brothers' death the flame of vengeance kindled, and then began a regime of overfeeding, physical exercises, and medical supervision, that would have made many a stouter heart quail.

Every week the family is present when the chest measure is taken.

"Just one more centimetre, and you'll be fit!" exclaims the enthusiastic father, while on the lashes of the smiling mother form two bright tears which trickle unheeded down her cheeks.

There reigns a supernatural enthusiasm among all these youths; an almost sacred fire burns in their eyes, their speech is pondered but passionate. They are so glad, so proud to go. They know but one fear—that of arriving too late.

"We don't want to belong to the Class that didn't fight."

And with it all they are so childlike and so simple—these heroes.

One afternoon, in a tea room near the Bon Marché, I noticed a soldier in an obscure corner, who, his back turned to us, was finishing with vigorous appetite, a plate of fancy cakes and pastry. (There was still pastry in those days—1917.)

"Good!" thought I. "I'm glad to see some one who loves cakes enjoying himself!"

The plate emptied, he waited a few minutes. Then presently he called the attendant.

She leaned over, listened to his whispered order, smiled and disappeared. A moment later she returned bearing a second well laden dish.

It was not long before these cakes too had gone the way of their predecessors.

I lingered a while anxious to see the face of this robust sweet tooth, whose appetite had so delighted me.

He poured out and swallowed a last cup of tea, paid his bill and rose, displaying as he turned about a pink and white beardless countenance, that might have belonged to a boy of fifteen—suddenly grown to a man during an attack of measles. On his breast was the *Medaille Militaire*, and the *Croix de Guerre*, with three palms.

This mere infant must have jumped from his school to an aeroplane. At any rate, I feel quite certain that he never before had been allowed out alone with sufficient funds to gratify his youthful passion for sweetmeats and, therefore, profiting by this first occasion, had indulged himself to the limit. Can you blame him?

VIII

To go from Le Mans to Falaise, from
Falaise to St. Lo; from St. Lo to Morlaix,
and thence to Poitiers would seem very easy
on the map, and with a motor, in times gone
by it was a really royal itinerary, so vastly
different and picturesque are the various
regions crossed. But now that gasolene is
handed out by the spoonful even to sanitary
formations, it would be just as easy for the
civilian to procure a white elephant as to
dream of purchasing sufficient "gas" to make
such a trip.

There is nothing to do but take the train,
and that means of locomotion not only requires time, but patience and considerable
good humour. Railway service in France has
been decidedly reduced, and while travelling
is permitted only to those persons who must
needs do so, the number of plausible motives
alleged has greatly augmented, with the result
that trains are crowded to the extreme limit.

To tell the truth, a good third of the population is always moving. For how on earth is one to prevent the parents of a wounded hero from crossing the entire country to see him, or deny them the right to visit a lad at his training camp?

This then accounts for the appearance of the Breton peasant's beribboned hat and embroidered waistcoat on the promenades of the Riviera, the Arlesian bonnet in the depths of Normandy, the Pyrenese cap in Lorraine.

All this heterogeneous crowd forms a long line in front of the ticket office, each one encumbered with a basket or a bag, a carpetsack or a bundle containing patés and sausages, pastry and pickles, every known local dainty which will recall the native village to the dear one so far away.

It is thus that from Argentan to Caën I found myself seated between a stout motherly person from Auvergne, and a little dark man from whose direction was wafted so strong an odour of garlic that I had no difficulty discerning from what region he hailed. Next to him were a bourgeois couple whose mourning attire, red eyes and swollen faces bespoke

plainly enough the bereavement they had just
suffered. Silent, indifferent to everything
and everybody, their hands spread out on their
knees, they stared into the ghastly emptiness,
vainly seeking consolation for their shattered
dream, their grief-trammelled souls.

A heavily built couple of Norman farmers
occupied the seats on either side of the door,
and then came a tall young girl and her
mother, a Belgian soldier, and finally .a
strange old creature wearing an antiquated
starched bonnet, a flowered shawl, and carrying an umbrella such as one sees but in en-
gravings illustrating the modes and customs
of the eighteenth century. She was literally
buried beneath a monumental basket which she
insisted upon holding on her knees.

Every available inch of floor space was covered with crocks and kits full of provisions,
and in the rack above our heads were so many
boxes and bundles, bags and bales, remaining
aloft by such remarkable laws of equilibrium
that I feared lest any moment they fall upon
our heads, and once this catastrophe occurred
there seemed to be little hope of extricating
oneself from beneath the ruins.

The conversation was opened by the Norman farmer who offered to relieve the little old woman of her basket and set it safely between his feet.

"Oh, non merci," she piped in a thin little wavering treble, and an inimitable accent which made it impossible to guess her origin.

"Oh, no, Monsieur, thank you," she continued. "It's full of cream tarts and cherry tarts, and custard pies made right in our own home. I'm taking them to my boy, and as we stayed up very late to make them so that they would be quite fresh, I should hate to have any of them crushed or broken. He did love them so when he was little!"

"Our son was just the same. As soon as he was able to eat he begged them to let him have some *brioche*. But his fever was too high when we got there, and he couldn't take a thing. 'That doesn't matter,' he said to his mother. 'Just the sight of them makes my mouth water, and I feel better already.'"

My Provençal neighbour could no longer resist. His natural loquaciousness got the better of his reserve.

"Well, the first thing my son asked for was

[177]

olives, so I brought him enough to last, as well
as some sausage which he used to relish. Oh,
if only I could bring him a little bit of our
blue sky, I'm sure he would recover twice as
quickly."

The mother of the young girl now sat forward and asked the Norman farmer's wife
where and how her son had been wounded.

"He had a splinter of shell in his left thigh.
He'd been through the whole campaign without a scratch or a day of illness."

The woman's eyes sparkled with pride and
tenderness.

The short man beside me, who informed me
he was a native of Beaucaire on the Rhone,
had one son wounded and being cared for in
a hospital at Caën, a second prisoner in Germany, and two sons-in-law already killed.

According to a letter which the dear old
flowered shawl spelled out to us word by
word, her grandson had been wounded in
seven different places, and had had one hand
and one leg amputated. But he hastened to
add that he was not worrying a bit about it.

The young girl's mother had one son in the
ranks, and a second, aged seventeen, had en-

listed and was about to leave for the front.
She and her daughter were on their way to
embrace him for the last time.

The Belgian soldier was just getting about
after an attack of typhoid fever, and the
motherly person on my left was travelling
towards her husband, a territorial of ripe years
whose long nights of vigil beneath bridges and
in the mud of the Somme had brought him
down with inflammatory rheumatism. Their
son, they prayed, was prisoner—having
been reported missing since the 30th of
August, 1914. This coarse, heavy featured
woman of the working classes, cherished her
offspring much as a lioness does her young.
She told us she had written to the President
of the Republic, to her Congressman, her
Senator, to the King of Spain, the Norwegian
Ambassador, to the Colonel of the Regiment,
as well as to all the friends of her son on whose
address she had been able to lay hand; and
she would keep right on writing until she obtained some result, some information. She
could not, would not, admit that her boy was
lost; and scarcely stopping to take breath she
would ramble on at length, telling of her hopes

and her disappointments to which all the compartment listened religiously while slowly the train rolled along through the smiling, undulating Norman country.

Each one did what he could to buoy up the mother's hopes.

The little Southerner seemed to possess a countless number of stories about prisoners, and he presently proceeded to go into minute detail about the parcels he sent to his own son, explaining the regulation as to contents, measures and weights, with so much volubility that the good soul already saw herself preparing a package to be forwarded to her long lost darling.

"You can just believe that he'll never want for anything—if clothes and food will do him any good. There's nothing on earth he can't have if only we can find him, if only he comes back to us."

And growing bolder as she felt the wealth of sympathy surrounding her, she looked over and addressed the woman in mourning, who at that moment smiled gently at her.

"We thought we knew how much we loved them, didn't we, Madame? But we'd never have realised how really deep it was if it hadn't been for this war, would we?"

The woman continued to smile sadly.

"More than likely you've got somebody in it too," persisted the stout Auvergnate, whose voice suddenly became very gentle and trembled a trifle.

"I *had* three sons. We have just buried the last one this morning."

All the faces dropped and a ghastly silence fell upon the group. Each one looked straight into the distance ahead of him, but the bond of sympathy was drawn still tighter, and in the moment of stillness that ensued I felt that all of us were communing with Sorrow.

Between Folligny and Lamballe, we were quite as closely huddled between three soldiers on furlough, a stout old priest, a travelling salesman, and a short gentleman with a pointed beard, a pair of eyeglasses and an upturned nose.

At one moment our train halted and waited an incredible length of time vainly whistling for the tower-man to lift the signal which impeded our progress.

The travelling salesman who was cross and weary finally left his seat, grumbling audibly.

"We'll never in the world get there on time. It's certain I shall miss my connection! What a rotten road! What management!"

"It's the war," murmered the priest pulling out a red checked handkerchief in which he buried his nose.

"You don't have to look far to see that," responded the other, still grumbling.

"Oh, it's plain enough for us all right. Those who are handling government jobs are the only fellows who don't know it, I should say."

"Bah! each of us has his troubles—each of us has his Cross to bear," murmured the Father by way of conciliation, casting his eyes around the compartment, much as he would have done upon the faithful assembled to hear him hold forth.

"Pooh! it's you priests who are the cause of all the trouble. It was you who preached and got the three year service law voted."

The poor Curate was fairly suffocated with surprise and indignation. He was so ruffled he could hardly find a word. In the meantime the travelling salesman taking advantage of his silence, continued:

"Yes, it was you and the financiers, and it's nothing to brag about either!"

The man with the upturned nose now wheeled about sharply. His blood was up and he strangely resembled a little bantam cockerel.

"Monsieur," he snapped, and his voice was clear and cutting, "if any one had a right to express a complaint on any subject whatsoever, it would certainly be the soldiers who are seated in this compartment. Now as they have said nothing, I cannot admit that you, a civilian, should take such liberties."

"But, Monsieur——"

"Yes, Monsieur, that's exactly what I mean, and as to the sentiments to which you have given voice they are as stupid as they are odious. We all know now that war was inevitable. The Germans have been preparing it for forty years."

"Monsieur!"

"Monsieur!"

The two glared fixedly at each other for an instant; the one was very red, the other ex-

[183]

tremely pale. Then they turned about and resumed their places in each corner. The priest
produced his breviary, the soldiers finished
a light repast composed of bread and cheese.

They were all three peasants, easily discernible from the way they slowly chewed and
swallowed, or caught up a crumb of cheese on
the point of their knives. They had sat silent
and listened to the outbursts without turning
an eyelash. Then presently one of them lifted
his head and addressing his companions in a
deep bass voice:

"Well," said he, "this makes almost two
days now that we've been on the way!"

"What have you got to kick about?" retaliated the other, shutting his knife and wiping
his mouth with the back of his hand. "You're
as well off here as you were in the trenches of
Bois Le Pretre, aren't you?"

The third one said nothing, but recommenced carving a cane which he had abandoned for an instant, and which he was ter-
minating with more patience than art, though
the accomplishment of his task seemed to give
him infinite pleasure.

As the commercial traveller had predicted,

we were hours late and in consequence missed our connection, but the platform of a station where two lines meet, offers, under such circumstances, so diverse and diverting a spectacle that we hardly regretted the delay. It is here that any one interested in physiognomy can best study and judge the masses, for it is as though the very texture from which France is woven were laid bare before him. This spectacle is constantly changing, constantly renewed, at times deeply moving. No face can be, or is, indifferent, in these days and one no longer feels himself a detached individual observer; one becomes an atom of the crowd, sharing the anxiety of certain women that one knows are on their way to a hospital and who half mad with impatience are clutching the fatal telegram in one hand, while with the fingers of the other they thrum on one cheek or nervously catch at a button or ornament of their clothing.

Or again one may participate in the hilarious joy of the men on furlough, who having discovered the pump, stand stripped to the waist, making a most meticulous toilet, all the while teasing a fat, bald-headed chap to whom

seem to have been on the way so long, and yet they are in no haste to arrive. Hunger gnawing them, they produce their provisions, and having seated themselves on their luggage, commence a repast, eating most slowly, the better to kill time while waiting for a train that refuses to put in an appearance.

The *buffet* is so full of noise, smoke and various other odours, that having opened the door one hesitates before entering. There is a long counter where everything is sold; bread, wine, cider, beer and lemonade; sandwiches, patés, fruit and sweetmeats. One makes his choice and pays in consequence. At the side tables the civilians are lost mid the mass of blue uniforms.

This is a station in Normandy, and for the boys of this region nothing can substitute a good big bowl of hot vegetable soup, seasoned with the famous *graisse normande* and poured over thin slices of bread, the whole topped off with a glass of cider or "pure juice" as they call it. It is a joy to see them seated about the board, their elbows on the table, their heads bent forward over the steaming bowl, whose savoury perfume as it rises to

MONSIEUR AMÉDÉ

their nostrils seems to carry with it a veritable ecstasy, if one were to judge by the beatific expression on every countenance.

"That goes right to the spot, doesn't it?"

From another table a voice responds:

"Yes, fellows, it's better than a kick in the shins, every time!"

The last mouthful gone, the cider bottles empty, they tighten the straps of their kit bags and rise regretfully from their seats.

"*Allez*. Off again, boys! *C'est la guerre!*" and they shuffle away humming and filling their pipes.

From the direction of the *buvette,* or *bar* comes noisy laughter followed by oaths. The uncertain voice of a seemingly intoxicated individual dominates all others. Yet nothing but soft drinks are sold.

"As the Colonel of the 243rd used to say," it continues, 'Soldiers of my regiment, repose upon your arms!' My arms are the bottle! My bottle and my wife are the only things worth while when I'm on furlough. I——"

His voice disappeared an instant, dimmed by the rising tumult. Then suddenly it broke forth anew—

"Attention! Present arms, here comes a coal scuttle. Now then,—flatten out on the back of your stomach!"

An instant later the man appeared at the threshold of the dining room.

He was a heavily built, big jointed, husky Norman farmer-soldier, with his helmet pulled down low over his eyes, so that the upper part of his face was completely hidden from view.

Suddenly he pushed it far back on his head, and casting a sweeping glance over the assembled diners, he called forth in stentorian tones that made every one turn around:

"Good evening, ladies and gentlemen!"

The cashier behind the counter, who evidently foresaw trouble, called out to him in shrill tones:

"You've made a mistake, go back to the *buvette*. You've nothing to do out here!"

Removing his helmet, the gallant knight made the lady a sweeping bow.

"Your servant, Madame. Your humble servant," he continued. "Cyprien Fremont, called Cyp for short."

"Did you hear what I said? Now then,

take yourself off," cried the ungracious adored one.

But the *poilu* was not to be so silenced.

Putting his hand to his heart and addressing the assembly:

"Ungrateful country!" he cried, "is it thus that you receive your sons who shed their blood for you?"

"That's all right, but go and tell it elsewhere. Go on, I say!"

"I've only got one more word to say and then it will be over."

But before he could utter that word his companions seized him and dragged him back from whence he came. As he disappeared from view, we heard him announce his intention of "doing some stunts"—which offer was apparently joyously accepted, followed by more laughter and several "dares."

Suddenly the most terrific noise of falling and breaking glass and china brought every one to his feet. Excited voices could be heard from the direction in which Cyprien had vanished. The army police dashed in, followed by the station master and all the employés. A lengthy discussion was begun, and having finished our dinner we left matters to adjust themselves and sauntered forth onto the platform.

Here we found our Cyprien surrounded by his companions, who were busy disinfecting and binding up the wounds that he had received when the china cabinet had collapsed upon him. One of the men poured the tincture of iodine onto a hand held fast by a friend. Two others were rolling a bandage about his head, while the patient, far from subdued, waved the only free but much enveloped hand that he possessed, beating time to the air that he was literally shouting and in whose rather bald verse the station master's wife was accused of the grossest infidelity.

"Shh! Cyprien," his friends enjoined; "shut up a bit, can't you?"

But it was no easy thing to impose silence upon Cyprien when he had made up his mind to manifest a thought or an opinion.

"You'll get us all into trouble, old man, see if you don't. Cut it out, won't you? See, here comes an officer."

The officer approached them.

"It's not his fault, sir," began one of the

fellows, before his superior had time to ask a question. "I assure you, it's not his fault. He's just back from Saloniki—his first furlough in a year, sir. It must have gone to his head. I swear he hasn't had anything but cider to drink, sir."

"But that's no excuse for making all this noise. Show me his military book!"

The officer took it, ran through the pages, and then approached Cyprien.

At the sight of the gold braid Cyprien stood up and saluted.

"Before you went to Saloniki, I see you fought at Verdun."

"Yes, sir."

"And at Beausejour?"

"Yes, sir."

"And Vauquois?"

"Yes, sir."

The eyes of the two veterans met; the officer's glance seeking to pierce that of the soldier in front of him. Then suddenly, in an irresistible burst of sympathy and respect, he thrust out his hand and caught up one of Cyprien's bandaged pair.

"I was there, too," was all he said.

[193]

Instantly sobered, our hero straightened up and literally crushed his superior's fingers in his mighty fist.

"Come with me," said the officer; "I know a place where you can rest until it's time to leave. And you boys here," said he turning towards them, "you'll see to it that he doesn't miss his train."

Night, inky black, fathomless night, had now settled about us. In the distance one could just discern the red and green signal lamps—at closer range the burning tip of a cigar or cigarette. The soldiers turned up their collars. The wind shifting to the north was piercing cold. One had to walk briskly up and down to avoid becoming chilled. Way at the other end of the platform the flare of fugitive matches revealed shadows moving about as though searching for something upon the ground.

"What are you looking for?"

"A third-class return ticket for Royan. That old lady over there has lost hers."

We turned about to see a poor old wrinkled soul, in her native Norman costume, wringing her hands in distress.

[194]

"What a misfortune! Oh dear, oh dear, what a misfortune! What will become of me now? What shall I do?"

And to each inquisitive newcomer she babbled forth her story of a wounded grandson whom she was on her way to visit. The curate and another man of her village had seen to her expenses. They had purchased her ticket and handed it to her with strict instructions not to lose it. For safety's sake she had knotted it in the corner of her handkerchief—and now it wasn't there!

The inquirer then examined her handkerchief, made her stand up and shake her clothing, turn her pockets inside out, empty her baskets and her handbag; and still not willing to trust the thoroughness of his predecessors he would begin looking all over the immediate vicinity, match in hand. So presently nearly two hundred men, forgetting their soreness and fatigue, were down on their knees scouring every nook and cranny. The sleepers were awakened, the drinkers routed out and put to work, scanning every inch of ground.

A loud and persistent ringing of an electric bell sounded on the air.

"Hey there, fellows!" called a tall Zouave. "Get together, the train is announced, and since we can't find grandma's ticket we can't leave the old girl alone in the dark, so come on, chip in—we'll make it up to her. She says it cost forty-two francs and ten centimes. Are you ready?"

And removing his helmet he started to make the rounds. In an instant coppers and silver rang in the steel recipient.

"Stop! that's enough."

They retired to count.

"Chic—there's some left over!"

"Never mind, she'll buy something for the kid with it."

Some one purchased the ticket.

"There now, grandma, a new ticket and enough to buy your boy a cake with, so you should worry! But as you're too young to travel alone, we're going to take you in with us. We just happen to be going your way. Here Ballut, Langlois! Quick there—take her baskets. Now then, don't let go my arm— here comes the train. Sh! don't cry, there's nothing to bawl about, we're all good fellows—

[196]

all of us got grandmas who'd make just as big fools of themselves if they had to travel."

And with infinite care and tenderness a dozen hands hoisted their precious burden into the dimly lighted wooden-benched compartment.

Yes, travelling in France under such circumstances is to me more interesting than ever, for when it is not one's fellow passengers who hold the attention, there are always those thousand and one outside incidents which the eye retains involuntarily. War factories and munition plants sprung from the ground as though by magic; immense training camps in course of construction, aviation fields over which so cleverly hover those gigantic, graceful war birds, who on catching sight of the train fly low and delight the astonished passengers by throwing them a greeting, or, challenging the engineer, enter into a race.

But above all, there is the natural panorama; that marvellous succession of hills and vales, hamlets and rivers, fields and gardens, so wonderfully harmonious beneath the pearl tinted sky. How it all charms and thrills, and

[197]

how near the surface is one's emotion on hearing a soldier voice exclaim:

"What a country to die for!"

. So the hours sped by, and at length we reached our destination. P—— is a flourishing little city, perched on the side of a rocky hill, with a broad landscape spreading out at its feet.

The best hotel is called "L'hotel des Hommes Illustres"—and its façade is adorned with the statues of the above mentioned gentlemen carved in stone. The proprietor, who built the edifice and paid the bill, having been sole judge in the choice of celebrities, the result is as astonishing as it is eclectic, and though absolutely devoid of beauty, thoroughly imposing.

We arrived before our luggage, which was conveyed by so old and puffy a horse that we considered it criminal not to leave our cab and finish the hill on foot. At the top of a monumental staircase we entered the hotel office, behind whose desk were enthroned two persons of most serious aspect; the one, stout and florid of complexion with a long nose and an allure worthy of Louis XIV, proudly bore upon her head such an extraordinary quantity of blond hair arranged in so complicated a fashion that I trembled to think of the time required to dress it. The other, sallow faced, with a long curved chin, might have been taken for a Spanish Infanta, pickled in vinegar and allspice.

The formality of greetings accomplished, princess number one produced a book in which we were to sign our names. The dignity and importance she attached to this ceremony would certainly not have been misplaced in a Grand Chamberlain preparing the official register for the signature of Peace preliminaries.

This, together with the manner in which she took note of our names, drying them with a spoonful of gold sand, gave me the illusion that I had just performed some important rite.

"One or two rooms?" she queried.

"One big room, Madame."

"With or without bath?" demanded the coadjutor, whose voice possessed a contralto quality utterly out of keeping with her pale blond hair and complexion.

"With bath, please."

A new register was opened. Both bent over it closely, each showing the other a different paragraph with her fore finger. Finally they murmured a few inaudible syllables and then shook their heads.

"Would you prefer number six or number fourteen?" finally asked the Infanta.

We looked at each other in astonishment, neither being superstitious about numbers, but it would have been painful to announce to these ladies that the matter was totally indifferent to us. They had been so condescending as to allow us a choice.

"Number six has a balcony and two windows. Number fourteen has one window and a bathroom," the princess informed us.

"But," continued the Infanta, "it is our duty to inform you that hot water has been forbidden by the municipal authorities, and that cold water is limited to two pitchers per person, per room."

I said I would take number six, which arrangement terminated the ladies' mental indecision, and seemed to please them greatly. They smiled benignly upon us.

The smaller one, whom I have called the coadjutor, because her throne was less elevated than the princess', put her finger on a button and a violent ringing broke the silence of the vast hallway. No one answered.

Three times she repeated the rings, with an imperious movement.

"Be kind enough to go and call Monsieur Amédé, Mademoiselle Laure."

On her feet, Mademoiselle Laure was even smaller than when seated. She crossed the vestibule, opened a door, and her strong voice resounded along an empty corridor from which issued the odour of boiling cauliflower.

"Monsieur Amédé!" she shouted anew, but not even an echo responded.

"Mademoiselle Laure, ask for the head waiter."

Mademoiselle Laure recrossed the vestibule and opening a door diametrically opposed to the other, called:

"Monsieur Balthazard!"

Monsieur Balthazard appeared, his shirt sleeves rolled up beyond his elbow, wiping his hands on a blue gingham apron. He was a little slim man who may have been sixty years old. A glass eye gave him a sardonic, comic or astonished air, according to the way he used his good one, which was constantly moving, at the same time that it was clear and piercing.

"Monsieur Balthazard—what an attire for a head waiter!"

"Madame, I was just rinsing the wine barrels."

"And how about the errands for the people in rooms twenty-four and twenty-seven."

A noise at the hall door attracted our attention. It was as though some one were making desperate and fruitless attempts to open it.

"There he is now," exclaimed Monsieur Balthazard. "I'll go and let him in. He's probably got his hands full."

Monsieur Amédé, literally swamped beneath his bundles, staggered into the vestibule. To the different errands confided to his charge by the hotel's guests had undoubtedly been added the cook's list, for an enormous cabbage and a bunch of leeks completely

[202]

hid his face, which was uncovered only as he let them fall to the ground.

When he had finally deposited his treasures, we discovered a small lad about fourteen or fifteen years of age, dressed in a bellboy's uniform which had been made for some one far more corpulent of stature. The sleeves reached far down over his hands, the tight fitting, gold buttoned jacket strangely resembled a cross between a bag and an overcoat, and though a serious reef had been taken in the trousers at the waist line, the legs would twist and sway—at times being almost as ample as those worn by the Turkish sultanas.

Our coachman now arrived with our luggage.

"Monsieur Amédé, take this luggage and accompany Monsieur and Madame to number six."

The child gathered up his new burden and started upstairs.

We followed, helping him pick up the various objects which successively escaped his grasp.

"Goodness, it seems to me you're awfully young to be doing such heavy work!"

[203]

"Oh," said he, wiping his brow, "I'm very lucky. My mother is cook here, and Monsieur Balthazard is my uncle. With old fat Julia, the maid, and Mathilde, the linen woman, we're all that's left. All the men have gone to war, and the women into the powder mills. We keep the hotel going, we do."

Monsieur Amédé was full of good will, and a desire to help me all he could. He explained to us that he was now building the solid foundation of a future whose glories he hardly dare think, so numerous and unfathomable did they seem. Unfortunately, however, we were obliged to note that he seemed little gifted for the various occupations to which he had consecrated his youth—and his glorious future— for in less than five minutes he had dropped a heavy valise on my toes, and upset an inkwell, whose contents dripped not only onto the carpet but onto one of my new bags. In trying to repair damages, Monsieur Amédé spoiled my motor veil and got several large spots on the immaculate counterpane, after which he bowed himself out, wiping his hands on the back of his jacket, assuring us that there was no harm done, that no one would scold us, nor think of asking us for damages.

We saw him again at dinner time, when disguised as a waiter he passed the different dishes, spilling sauce down people's necks, tripping on his apron and scattering the handsome pyramids of fruit hither and yon. Lastly he took a plunge while carrying out an overloaded tray, but before any one could reach him he was on his feet, bright and smiling, exclaiming:

"I'm not hurt. No harm done. I'll just sweep it up. It won't stain."

In the meantime quiet, skilful Uncle Balthazard strained every nerve in a herculean effort to keep his temper and serve thirty persons all at once.

It was touching to hear the old man murmur, "Gently, boy—go gently," as his youthful protégé stumbled from one blunder to another. "Go gently, you can be so clever when you're not in a hurry!"

Monsieur Amédé almost caused us to miss the train next evening in spite of the numerous warnings from the princess behind the desk, who had arranged the hour of our departure. That brilliant young man who had

been sent ahead with our luggage was no-
where to be found when our train was announced. My husband, a woman porter, a soldier on furlough who knew him, started out to
scour the immediate surroundings of the station, finally locating him in a backyard near the
freight depot, his hands in his pockets, ex-
citedly following a game of nine-pins at which
a group of convalescent African soldiers was
playing.

Of course he immediately explained that
there was no harm done since the train was
twenty minutes late, and when finally it arrived
and he handed our baggage into the compartment, he accidentally let slip a little wooden box
containing an old Sevres vase, which I had
purchased at an antiquity dealer's that very
morning.

He picked it up, exclaiming:

"Lucky it's not fragile."

And lifting his cap, on whose visor one
might read "Hotel des Hommes Illustres," he
cheerfully wished us a *Bon voyage.*

IX

Before the war it used to be Aunt Rose's
victoria that met us at the station; a victoria
drawn by a shiny span and driven by pompous
old Joseph, the coachman, clad in a dark green,
gold-buttoned livery and wearing a cockade on
his hat. Aunt Rose's coachman, and the Swiss
at Nôtre Dame were classed among the curi-
osities of the city, as could be attested by the
numerous persons who hastened to their doorstep to see the brilliant equipage pass by.

But this time we found the victoria relegated
beside the old "Berline" which Aunt Rose's
great-grandmother had used to make a jour-
ney to Italy; the horses had been sent out to
the farm, where they were needed, and Joseph,
fallen from the glory of his box, attired in a
striped alpaca vest, and wearing a straw hat,
half civilian, half servant, seemed a decidedly
puffy old man, much aged since our last visit.

"Monsieur and Madame will be obliged to

take the omnibus. Will Monsieur kindly give me the baggage check?"

Then as I fumbled in my purse—

"Monsieur and Madame will find many changes, I fear."

But in spite of his prophecy to us there seemed little difference. The rickety old omnibus rattled and bumped noisily over the pointed cobble pavements, the tiny city merely seemed asleep behind its drawn blinds and its closed shutters. At the corner of the square in front of the château the old vegetable vendor still sold her products seated beneath her patched red cotton parasol; the Great Dane watchdog lay in exactly the same place on the tinker's doorstep. Around the high church tower the crows circled and cawed as usual, while the bell of its clock which, as we passed, slowly struck three, was echoed by the distant hills with the same familiar sound.

The omnibus deposited us at the entrance to the big roomy edifice which Aunt Rose called "home."

The broad façade, evenly pierced by its eighteen long French windows, had a genial, inviting appearance, while the soft rose colour of the bricks, the white stone trimming, the iron balconies, mingled here and there with bas-reliefs and sculptures, were in perfect harmony with the tall slanting slate roof and majestic chimneys, the whole forming one of those delightful ensembles constructed by local architects during the 17th century for the pleasure and comfort of a large French bourgeois family.

Aunt Rose herself, leaning upon an ivory-headed cane, but bright eyed and alert as ever, awaited us at the top of the steps. From her we soon learned that we had missed our friends the M.'s by but a day, and that little André, son of our cousins in Flers, had announced his visit for the following Monday.

At this point Friquet, her old Pomeranian favourite, crept down from his cushion and approached us.

"He doesn't bark any more, so you know he must be getting old," smiled Aunt Rose, caressing her pet.

"My poor Victoire is getting on, too, I fear. Her nephew is stone blind since the battle of the Marne. Joseph has lost two of his grandsons; of course, he didn't tell you—he doesn't want any one to speak of it—but he's very much upset by it. Nicholas and Armandine do nothing but worry about their poor little Pierre, who hasn't given a sign of life for three months now—so I fear you will have to be very patient and very indulgent guests."

The delightful old lady led us to our room, "the psyche room" we, the youngsters, used to call it on account of the charming grisaille wall paper, dating from the end of the Empire period, and representing in somewhat stiff but none the less enchanting manner the amorous adventures of that goddess.

I have always had a secret feeling that many a time, urged by her confessor, Madame de C. had been upon the point of obliterating or removing those extremely chaste nude images. But at the last moment rose up the horror of voluntarily changing anything in the homestead, transforming a whole room that she always had known thus, and perhaps the unavowed fear of our ridicule and reproach, had made her renounce her project.

"Brush up quickly, and come right down to

tea. We've got so many things to talk over. You've so much to tell me!"

So a quarter of an hour later, tea-cup in hand, we must needs go into the details of our trips, inform her of our hopes and fears, tell of all the different things we had seen—what America was going to do—what it had already accomplished. And with her marvellously quick understanding, her vivacious intelligence, the old lady classified the facts and the anecdotes, asked us to repeat dates and numbers, that she might the better retain them in her splendid memory.

All through dinner and the long evening she plied us with questions, kept the conversation running along the same lines, returning now and then to a certain theme, or certain figures, and asking us to go into even more detail.

"I know I'm an abominable old egoist," at length she apologised. "But you'd forgive me if only you realised how much happiness your stories will bring, and to how many people. I imagine that you haven't had much time for correspondence with our family—but that's all an old woman like myself is good for these days."

"Our family" consisted in relationship to the 'nth degree of all the H's, de C's, B's and F's that were then in existence, some of them such distant cousins that Aunt Rose herself would never have recognised them had they met. And besides these people there were her friends, her servants, her farmers, possibly a group of three hundred persons with whom the good soul corresponded, giving news of the ones to the others, announcing misfortunes or joys—a living link between us all.

Left a widow when still quite young, Aunt Rose had lived with and respected the memory of her husband. Though she had had many an offer, she had never cared to remarry. But unable to stand the damp climate of Normandy, she had returned to her family homestead in this little city of the Bourbonnais, in whose suburbs she possessed quite a fortune in farm lands. Alone in the world, with no immediate family, she had devoted herself not only to her own, but to her husband's relatives. Her home had always been the *havre de grace,* known and venerated by them all; a meeting place for reconciliation between persons whose self-control had escaped them; the shelter for prodigal and repentant sons who awaited the forgiveness of their justly wrathful sires; the comforting haven that seemed to assuage the pangs of departure and bereavement. But above all it was the one spot for properly celebrating family anniversaries, announcing engagements, and spending joyous vacations.

The war had been the cause of a great deal of hard work in this respect.

"Why, I receive more letters than a State functionary," Aunt Rose informed me when I came upon her early the next morning, already installed behind her huge flat-topped desk, her tortoise-shell spectacles tipped down towards the end of her very prominent nose.

"For nearly four years I've been writing on the average of twenty letters a day and I never seem to catch up with my correspondence. Why, I need a secretary just to sort out and classify it. You haven't an idea the different places that I hear from. See, here are your letters from the United States. Léon is in the Indo-Chinese Bank in Oceania. Albert is mobilised at Laos, Quentin in Morocco. Jean-Paul and Marcel are fighting at Saloniki; Emilien in Italy. Marie is Superior in a convent at Madrid; Madeline, Sister of Charity at Cairo. You see I've a world-wide correspondence.

"Look," she continued, opening a deep drawer in one side of her desk, "here are the letters from my *poilus* and, of course, these are only the answered ones. The dear boys just love to write and not one of them misses a week without doing so. I'm going to keep them all. Their children may love to have them some day."

Then she opened a smaller drawer, and my eye fell upon a dozen or fifteen packages, all different in size and each one enveloped in white tissue paper, carefully tied about with grey silk ribbon.

"These were written by our dear departed," she said simply.

In an instant they passed before my eyes, those "dear departed." Big, tall William, so gay and so childish, he who used to play the ogre or the horse, or anything one wished: a person so absolutely indispensable to their games that all the little folk used to gather

FLOCKING TO READ THE COMING
COMMUNIQUÉ IN A LITTLE
FRENCH CITY

beneath his window early in the morning, crying in chorus: "Uncle William! Uncle William! do wake up and come down and play!"

Jean-François, the engineer; Philippe, the architect; Honoré, whom we dubbed "Deshonoré," because he used always to return empty-handed when we went hunting together. Gone, gone forever!

Aunt Rose picked up one of the smaller packages.

"These were from little Jacques." And two bright tears trembled on her lashes.

"You remember him, of course, my dear. He was an orphan, he never knew his mother. I always supposed that is what made him so distant and reserved. Jean, his guardian, who is very severe, used to treat him as he did his own children—scolding him often about his indolence, his lack of application to his studies.

"I used to have him here with me during his vacations. He loved this old house—and I knew it. Sometimes when you would all start out for some excursion I'd see him coming back towards the gate:

" 'You're not going with them then, Jacques?'

" 'No, thank you, Aunt Rose, it's so nice in your drawing-room.'

."When he was just a little baby I often wanted to take him onto my lap and laugh and play with him. But he was so cold and distant! A funny little mite, even with boys of his own age. Nobody seemed to understand him exactly; certain people even thought that his was a surly nature.

"He spent his last furlough here, and I found quite a change in him. He was more robust and tanned. A splendid looking fellow, and I was so proud of him.

" 'Aunt Rose,' he asked even before we embraced, 'is there any one else stopping with you?'

" 'Why no, child, and I'm afraid you'll find the house very empty. If only I'd known you were coming I most certainly should have invited your cousins.'

" 'Oh, I'm so glad you didn't! I much prefer being alone with you.'

"He came and went in the house, but never could be persuaded to go outside the yard. I should have loved to have taken him with me and shown his War Cross to some of my old friends. But he wouldn't hear of it.

" 'Pooh!' he would laugh when I would suggest such a thing. 'If ever they come near me I'll tell them I've got "trench pest"—and then you'll see them clear out.'

"He went down in the kitchen and I'd hear him pottering around. I never knew him so gay and happy.

" 'Tante Rose, I'm going to sing you "La Madelon" and the "Refrain de la Mitraille." It was Planchet, the tinsmith, who composed it!'

"He'd sit for hours in that big blue armchair, blinking at the fire, and then suddenly he'd come to earth and explain:

" 'Aunt Rose, what a pleasure to be here.'

"When finally he had to go back, he caught me and whispered in my ear, as I kissed him:

" 'Next time, Tante, you promise me not to invite any one, won't you?'

"Poor child, he will never come back, and his friend Planchet, the tinsmith, saw him fall with a bullet through his heart. It was he who wrote me the sad news.

"Well, my dear, what mystery the soul hides

[217]

within itself! In one of the cupboards of the room he occupied I found two note books and a diary filled with verses he had never shown to any one, never admitted having written. How little we guessed what he was about when we scolded him for his indolence and inattention. If you only knew what accents, what harmonious phrases he found to depict the shades of our trees, the rippling of the river, the perfume of the flowers and his love for us all.

"There is a whole chapter devoted to the old homestead. He seemed to feel everything, divine everything, explain everything. None of us understood him. There is no use pretending we did. Not one among us would ever have guessed that so splendid and delicate a master of the pen lived and moved amongst us."

Aunt Rose looked straight out onto the sunlit court, the great tears trickling down her cheeks.

For a long time neither of us spoke.

Like its mistress, Aunt Rose's home lives to serve the war. The culinary realm is always

[218]

busily engaged preparing *patés* and *galantines, rillettes* and sausages. "For our boys," is the answer almost before the question is put. "They're so glad to get home-made dainties, and are always clamouring for more—no matter how much you send!

"Since they must eat preserved food, we might as well send them something we make ourselves, then we're sure it's the best. Why, I'd be ashamed to go out and buy something and send it off without knowing who had handled it." This was the cook's idea of patriotism, which I shared most heartily, having at one time had nothing but "bully beef" and dried beans as constant diet for nearly a fortnight.

The coachman and inside man sealed the crocks and tins, prepared and forwarded the packages.

"Oh, there's one for everybody! Even the boys of the city who haven't got a family to look after them. They must be mighty glad Madame's alive. We put in one or two post cards, views of the town. That cheers them up and makes them feel they're not forgotten here in R——."

One afternoon on descending into the kitchen we beheld two sturdy looking fellows seated at table and eating with ravenous appetite. One was an artilleryman who had but a single arm, the other a *chasseur,* whose much bandaged leg was reposing upon a stool.

"They are wounded men on convalescent leave," explained Armandine. "The poor fellows need a little humouring so that they'll build up the quicker, and an extra meal surely can't hurt!"

This was certainly the opinion of the two invalids who had just disposed of a most generous bacon omelet, and were about to dig into a jar of *paté.*

Armandine and Nicholas watched them eat with evident admiration, fairly drinking up their words when between mouthsful they would stop for breath and deign to speak. Their rustic eloquence was like magic balm poured onto a constantly burning, ulcerated sore.

"Your son? Why, of course, he'll turn up!" the artilleryman assured them.

"But he hasn't written a line!"

"That's nothing. Now just suppose that correspondence is forbidden in his sector for the time being."

"I know, but it's three months since we heard from him. We've written everywhere, to all the authorities, and never get any returns—except now and then a card saying that they're giving the matter their attention. That's an awfully bad sign, isn't it?"

"Not at all, not at all," chimed in the *chasseur*. "Why, some of the missing have been found in other regiments, or even in the depots, and nobody knows how they got there.

"Three months? Why, that's not long. After the battle of the Marne my poor old mother had them say Heaven knows how many masses for the repose of my soul; for four months and three days she never heard a thing of me, and I'd written her regularly every week.

"Yes, and what are you going to do if the letter carrier gets killed, or the Boche locate the mail waggon on the road every other delivery? Nobody's going to inform you of the accident."

"And that does happen often?"

[221]

"Almost every day."

"Quite a common occurrence; there's nothing for you to worry about yet, really now."

So "hope springs eternal" in the breasts of the bereaved parents, whose smile gradually broadens out into a laugh when the artilleryman recounts some grotesque tale, and gives his joyous nature free rein.

The convalescents who came to this particular city must have recuperated in the minimum of time, if *régime* had anything to do with the re-establishment. In every house the cloth was always on the table, the door open in sign of welcome.

"Come in and have a bite with us," people would call to them as they passed by.

Certain among them were being treated for severe cases and had been in the city a long time. The townspeople were proud of their progress and their cure, almost as proud as of their notary, who on leaving for the front was only a second lieutenant, but now had command of a battalion of *chasseurs*. Nor must one forget Monsieur de P.'s son, cited for bravery among the aces, and least of all ignore Monsieur Dubois, who having lost both sons, shut up his house, settled his business and without telling any one went off and enlisted as a simple private at sixty-two years of age.

In coming to this distant little city I had sought to find repose for my somewhat shattered nerves; dared hope for complete rest beneath this hospitable, sympathetic roof. But the war was everywhere. Yes, far from the sound of the guns one's eyes are spared the spectacles of horror and desolation, but there is not a soul who for a single instant really escapes the gigantic shiver that has crept over all the world. Out here, far removed from the seat of events, life necessarily becomes serious and mournful. The seemingly interminable hours lend themselves most propitiously to reflections, foster distress and misgivings, and one therefore feels all the more keenly the absence of the dear ones, the emptiness due to the lack of news.

There are but two moments when real excitement ripples the apparent calm of the little city; one in the morning when the paper boy announcing his approach by blowing his brass horn, runs from door to door distribut-

elm that shaded one corner of the square. Now and again a woman would leave her companions and wiping the perspiration from her brow, approach this humble cradle, lift her infant in her arms, and seeking a secluded spot, give it suckle.

I cannot tell how long I stood watching this wonderful rustic spectacle, so rich in tone and colouring, so magnificent in its simplicity, so harmonious in movement. There was no undue noise—every motion seemed regulated, the work accomplished without haste but with an impressive thoroughness. Here then was the very source of the country's vitality. Elsewhere the war might crush and destroy lives, cities and possessions, but this was the bubbling spring-head from whence gushed forth, unrestrained, the generative forces; stronger than war, stronger than death, life defiantly persistent. And I was seized with an immense pride, an unlimited admiration for these noble, simple women of France who had had the courage to set forth such a challenge!

For it is the women who have done it, of that there can be no doubt.

The census indicates that in 1914 the total

MAXENCE

number of inhabitants within this little village was seven hundred and fifty. Of these, one hundred and forty men were mobilised, and forty-five have already been killed. The masculine element, therefore, has been reducd to a minimum.

Thevenet, the carpenter, grocery man and choir leader, gifted with a strong voice and a shock of curly black hair, but lame in both legs, is certainly, when seated behind his counter, the noblest specimen of the stronger sex that the village possesses.

His pupil, disciple and companion, called Criquet, is, as his pseudonym indicates, extremely small of stature, and though he regularly presents himself before the draft boards, he has invariably been refused as far too small to serve his country in the ranks.

Of course, there are quite a number of sturdy old men, who have had ample occasion to do their bit by helping their daughters or their sons' wives on their farms. So in the village itself there remains hardly any one.

Old man Magnier is so bent with rheumatism that each movement is accompanied by an alarming cracking of his bones, and one is

tempted to ask him not to stir for fear of suddenly seeing him drop to pieces, as would an
antiquated, over-dry grandfather clock, on
being removed from a long stay in the garret.

Monsiau, the inn-keeper, is ready and willing to do almost anything but he is so terribly stout that the slightest physical effort
causes him to turn purple and gasp for breath.
He therefore remains seated, nodding like a
big Buddha, half dozing over the harangues of
his friend Chavignon, the tailor, whose first
name, by the way, is Pacifique. But in order
to belie this little war-like appellation, Chavignon spends most of the time he owes to the
trade dreaming of impossible plans and preparing ghastly tortures, to which the Kaiser
shall be submitted when once we have caught
him.

Bonnet, the hardware dealer, in spite of his
seventy-eight years, comes and goes at a lively
pace—coughing, grumbling, mumbling—always in a hurry, though he never has anything
special to attend to.

And finally there is Laigut; Laigut whom
one consults when at his wits' end, simply because he knows everything in general, and

nothing in particular, his knowledge covering all the arts and sciences as resumed in the Grand Encyclopedia. He is a little man with spectacles, and a short grey beard, costumed winter and summer alike in the same suit of worn brown velvet, a rabbit skin cap on his head, his feet shoved into wooden sabots.

His reputation before the war was not what one would call spotless. His passion for fowl (other people's on principle) had led to his being strongly suspected. He was a poacher, as well, always ready to bring you the hare or the pike you needed, at a fixed date and hour, more especially when the shooting and fishing seasons were closed.

His was one of those hidden geniuses which the war had revealed. Otherwise we should never on earth have suspected him of being so capable. But be it requested that he repair a sewing machine, a bicycle or a watch; sharpen a pair of scissors, put in a pane of glass, make over mattresses, shear a horse, a dog or a human, paint a sign, cover an umbrella, kill a pig or treat a sprain, Laigut never hesitates, Laigut is always found competent. Add to this his commerce in seeds and herbs, his talent

[233]

for destroying snakes and trapping moles, the fact that he is municipal bell ringer and choir boy, and you will have but a feeble idea of the activities of this man whose field seems so unlimited.

In a little old shed behind his house he carefully stores the innumerable and diverse objects which are confided to his care, and contrary to what one might suppose, he bears no malice for the lack of esteem bestowed upon him in times gone by. Not at all. His breadth of character is equalled only by the diversity of his gifts. From time to time a fowl may still disappear, but none save *Maître Renard* is now accused. In these days there are so many foxes about!

If I may seem to have gone deep into detail concerning these people it is only because I am anxious to make better understood what life means in a village without men. That is to say without valid men who care for the cattle, steer the plough, keep the furrows of equal depth and straight as a die; rake, hoe and sow; reap, harvest and carry the heavy burdens, in fact, perform all the hard, fatiguing labour that the upkeep of the soil requires.

And yet, in spite of their absence, not a foot of ground has been neglected. The cattle are robust and well cared for, the harvests reaped and brought to cover, the taxes and the rents have been paid, and down under the piles of linen in those big oak cupboards lie many blue bank notes, or several bonds of the National Defense. And France has crossed the threshold of her fifth year of war.

To whom is this due? The women.

There were no training schools to teach them how to sow or reap—no kindly advisors to take the husbands' places and tell them what animals to keep and feed, at what time to sell, or at what price. They had to learn from hard experience, taxing their intuition and great common sense to the utmost.

And with it all they are so shy and modest; at heart a little bit ashamed when you speak to them in terms of admiration for what they have done.

"We didn't really know what to do at the end of that first year when we found there wasn't any one to take care of the ground," explained Julie Laisné, who lives just behind Aunt Rose.

"I would have tried to plough, been glad to do it, but I was afraid the others would make fun of me," said Anna Troussière.

"That's just the way I felt about it," exclaimed Julie. "I nearly went crazy when I knew time was flying, winter coming, and no wheat in. I've no doubt it was the same with all the others. Then one day the news ran round like lightning that Anna was out ploughing her fields, with her kid and her grandfather to help her. Nobody took the time to go and see if it was true. Each one got out her plough. Of course, the first furrows were not very straight, but soon we got used to it, and Lord, how we laughed over my first attempts, when my husband came home the next fall on furlough."

I wish that some great master of the pen might paint in words as simple as the Golden Legend, in stanzas as pure as the Litanies of the Holy Virgin, the picture of this little Julie, up and about with the first rays of dawn, always hard at work, and whom when night has closed in I have often come upon, bending over beneath her tallow candle, writing to the dear one at the front. To this task as to all

the others she concentrates her every effort
and attention, anxious that no news be forgotten,—news which is as fresh and naïve as the
events and the nature that inspires it. "The
sow has had twelve little pigs, the donkey has
a nail in its hoof, little Michel has a cold, and
butter now sells for forty-three sous the
pound. "

Her farm is too small and brings in too little for her to dream of taking on some one to
help. But she keeps three cows, and three
calves; a dozen or two pigs, a donkey and all
the chickens she can afford to feed. Forty
acres is quite a responsibility for so small a
person, and it requires lots of courage to replace the missing muscle, to till the soil, care
for the kitchen garden and the animals, and
send three small children off to school on time,
all of them washed and combed, without a hole
in their stockings or a spot on their aprons. It
needs something more than courage to be
able to sing and dissimulate one's anxieties, to
hide in one corner of that envelope that will be
opened by him "Out there," a little favourite
flower, tenderly cared for, nursed to maturity.

"Bah!" she laughs as I sympathise. "It

might be bad if one were all alone in his troubles. But we're all in the same boat, down here!"

Yes, all of them have done their duty—more than their duty, the impossible. In other villages it is just the same—in other Provinces. From one end to the other of France such marvels have been accomplished that the government decided that so much devotion merited recompense.

So one fine morning a motor was seen to stop in front of the Café Lacroix, a gentleman in uniform (some say it was the Préfet) accompanied by two other men, got down and walked over to the town hall that is near the church.

A few moments later Criquet was dispatched on bicycle to Anna Troussière's and Claudine Charpin's, with orders to bring them back with him.

He soon returned accompanied by the two frightened creatures, who fearing ill news had not unrolled their sleeves nor removed the handkerchief from their heads, but jumped on their bicycles and hastened to the town hall.

Then suddenly the gentleman in uniform

[238]

appeared on the steps, made them a little speech, and stepping down pinned a medal on their heaving breasts. He thrust a diploma which bore their names into their trembling fingers, shook hands with them most cordially, and mounting in his car, drove away in a cloud of dust.

Every one, much excited, gathered around the two women. The medals were handed about, commented upon.

"Beautiful," exclaimed Criquet who is something of a wag. "I think they're made of bronze. Too bad they're not chocolate so you might give us all some."

"Claudine," said Anna Troussière, "it's time we went home if we don't want to be teased to death. Goodness, if only we'd known, we might have brushed up a bit!"

But the incident did not end there. The government, anxious to show its gratitude, offered to send them help, in the shape of war prisoners. The proposition was tempting. A bourgeois who had several big farms said he would accept four. This almost caused a revolution. The four Germans were quartered in a shed and an old territorial mounted guard over them.

"They were good fellows," Julie explained when she told me the story. "Hard workers too. Very kind to the animals and understanding everything about a farm. I don't know—I used to have a funny feeling when I saw them. But, poor souls, I don't suppose they wanted the war, they'd probably have much rather been home and yet they were as obliging as could be. Always ready to lend a hand when there was a hard job to be tackled.

"They made rather a good impression, and two or three of our women farmers had almost decided to send for some. Well, this lasted until the next Sunday. As they were all catholics, of course they came to church, and were seated on the first bench, with their sentinel at the end. Everything went finely until the Curate got up to preach, first reading the announcements for the week. When he asked that prayers be said for Jules Lefoulon and Paul Dupont, both from our parish and both killed on the Field of Honour, and we looked up we could see the four Boche sitting calmly in front of us—I can't tell you what it meant! Every one was weeping. Of course, we didn't let *them* feel it. They saluted every one most politely, you could almost see that they weren't bad men—but every one said, 'No, none of their help needed. We've got on without them up till now. I fancy we can see it through.' "

Even Madame Fusil, the baker, who was in most urgent need of assistance, resolved to be equal to her task alone. It is her little daughter who delivers the bread to all the numerous patrons, quite a complicated undertaking for so young a child, who must drive her poor old nag and his load down many a bumpy side path. One can hear her little voice all over the country side. "Here Jupiter—get up, I say."

I met her one morning in the Chemin du Moulin, whip in hand, pulling old Jupiter by the bridle. But Jupiter had decided to take a rest. Nothing could make him budge, nothing, neither cries nor complaints, sweetmeats nor menaces. Jupiter was as determined as he was obstinate.

The unfortunate child was red with indignation, almost on the verge of tears.

"Oui, oui," she fairly sobbed, "he just

ought to be sent to the front. That would teach him a lesson. He does it on purpose, I do believe. He knows well enough I'll be late to school! It's already half past seven. I've got three more deliveries to make, and must take him home and unharness him!"

"What time did you start out, child?"

"Why, four o'clock as usual, Madame. But I'm sure to be late this morning."

I promised that as I was passing by the school I would step in and tell Madame Dumont, the head mistress, the reason of her tardiness. She felt much better after that, and presently our combined efforts got Jupiter to move.

True to my word I sought out Madame Dumont, and found the good woman already extremely busy at this early hour.

A peasant mother and her three children all arrayed in their Sunday best, were grouped together at one end of the garden, smiling blandly into the lens of a camera which the school mistress set up and prepared to operate.

"There—that's it—smile! Click! It's all over. Now then, Magloire, climb up on a chair.

[242]

Hold yourself quite straight, dear, so your papa will see how much you've grown."

Magloire was photographed with her nose in the air, her mouth wide open, her other features registering the most complete lunacy. Joseph, her brother, at whom they fairly shrieked in order to make him smile, produced the most singular contortion of the mouth that I have ever seen, which denoted an extreme gift for mimicry, rare in so young a child.

Little Marie was taken on her mother's lap, and I thought of the ecstasy of the brave fellow to whom one day the postman would bring the envelope containing the glorious proofs. With what pride he will show them to his companions, how he will gloat over his Magloire and his Joseph, his petite Marie and his *bonne femme*. Then, drawing away from the others, he will study them again, each one in turn. Nights when on duty, those cold nights of vigil, way out there in Saloniki, when fatigue and homesickness will assail him, he will slip his hand down into his pocket, and his rough fingers will touch the grease stained envelope that contains the cherished faces of his dear ones.

[243]

It all recalled other powder-blackened hands clenched forever about soiled remnants of envelopes, from which protruded the edge of a precious photograph. A shiver ran down my spine as the brave mother and her three little ones passed by me on their way to change their clothes—assume their humble dress.

"*Merci, Madame Dumont. Merci bien.*"

"At your service, Madame Lecourt." And Madame Dumont turned to examine her mail. Rather voluminous in size, but with the Mayor, his substitute, and her husband at the front, she had become town clerk, and the quantity of paper and printed matter a village like this daily receives, is quite unbelievable. Quickly the little school mistress ran through the envelopes, finally breathing a deep sigh of relief.

"Ah, nothing this mail, thank Heaven!"

"Why, what were you expecting?"

"Oh, I wasn't expecting anything, but I live in terror of finding that fatal official bulletin announcing the death of some man in our community. Each time I leave the house, the eyes of every living soul are fairly glued to me.

[244]

The women here love me, I know, and yet I feel that I frighten them.

"If on going out I start up the road, those who live below here breathe again, relieved. You cannot imagine the tricks I must resort to in order not to arouse false suspicions. Then, as soon as I open their door they know the reason of my coming, and what poor miserable creatures I often take in my arms and try vainly to console.

"Ah, Madame, the wives you can cope with, say things to, put their babies in their arms. But the mothers, Madame, the mothers!"

"And no one complains, Madame Dumont?"

"No one, Madame, they all know that we've *got* to win this war."

All along the road home I walked slowly, lost in reverie. But I had no time for musing after my arrival, for Aunt Rose met me at the doorstep, a small boy by her side.

"Listen, my dear," she cooed, "I've a great favour to ask you. Would you mind walking around to the farms and telling them that Maxence will be here to-morrow morning? His little boy has just come over to tell me."

The coming of Maxence produced an inde-